Make Your Boss Happy

Published by :
Lotus Press Publishers & Distributors

Make Your Boss Happy

Sharad Paul

4735/22, Prakash Deep Building
Ansari Road, Darya Ganj,
New Delhi - 110002

Lotus Press Publishers & Distributors
Unit No. 220, 2nd Floor, 4735/22, Prakash Deep Building,
Ansari Road, Darya Ganj, New Delhi-110002
Ph.: 23280047, 41325510, 98118-38000
• E-mail : lotuspress1984@gmail.com
www.lotuspress.co.in

Make Your Boss Happy

ISBN: 81-8382-179-0

Printed & Published by : **Lotus Press Publishers & Distributors,** New Delhi-02

Preface

The relationship you have with your boss is very important on both a professional and a personal level. It can have a significant influence on your day-to-day job satisfaction as well as your long-term career success. The relationship is also important to your boss who is counting on you, and your colleagues, to satisfy customers, meet deadlines and achieve objectives.

But keeping this relationship healthy and productive is not about managing your boss: it is about understanding them, and you, and then choosing to behave in a way that gets the best results for you, your boss and the organisation. Only by understanding your mutual needs, styles, expectations, strengths and weaknesses can you develop a relationship that works for both of you.

Everyone knows how important it is to have a good relationship with their boss, but not everyone knows how to go about doing this. There are many things you can do that are completely legitimate and won't make you look like a suck up. This book provides you the simple tips and techniques to make your boss happy. It is a step-by-step guide to help career-minded men and women understand their boss's psychological profile. There is also advice on dealing with the boss from hell, and coping with common problems.

Author

Contents

1

Ways to Make Your Boss Like You

Your relationship with your boss is one of the most important factors in achieving a successful career. You can't expect your boss to change to accommodate you. Even if you feel your boss is in the wrong—or unreasonable, or tyrannical—the only behaviour you control is your own.

The single-most important thing to make sure your boss likes you is to do an excellent job. Perhaps you do a great job—phenomenal, even—and the boss just doesn't notice. Or perhaps you think you're doing a great job, but not according to your boss's wishes. What you think of as perfect and what he/she thinks of as perfect may be very different.

In order to get on your boss's good side, you must see yourself from their point of view. Here are a few ways to do that.

1. *Listen.* This is the biggest breakdown in most office environments—people don't truly listen to one another. A fast-track to a boss who hates you is failing to properly follow instructions. Next time you have face-time with your boss, be prepared to truly listen. Be in the moment—don't allow your mind to wander to what you'll say in response.

Write the important stuff down: deadlines, dates, figures, and even instructions that might seem simple at the time. Most people think their memories are better than they actually are. But all it takes is a few phone calls or e-mails in between to wipe a conversation from your memory. It doesn't hurt to write stuff down—worst case scenario, you won't need it. Best case, you do need it, and find that you're remembering it wrong, so you correct your mistake before the boss sees it.

2. *Ask questions.* Never assume things. Never assume how things are done or need to be done. When you are not clear always ask. You probably think, wouldn't that make me look bad? Well, what is worst? Because you assumed you got the work wrong and spend more time correcting it or asking to clarify?
3. *But don't be a pest.* Unless your boss is a micro-manager, some things are up to your discretion. Don't interrupt meetings or conference calls to ask about a font for the memo or go over instructions he's/she's already given you. Be self-sufficient.
4. *Make him/her look good.* Now, that doesn't mean you take blame for things that go wrong. It can be something as easy as preparing the background to a meeting he/she is attending. In this case, ensure that she has the pertinent information needed to have a productive meet.
5. *Take initiative.* Asking when you do not know does not mean that you cannot take initiatives. In fact, you should learn to take initiatives when the need arise or when the opportunity presents itself. Is there something that can be done better or should be attended to but no one found the time to attend to it. Ask to be the one in charge and make sure you see through the initiative you have taken.

6. *Be an ever present help.* Be there whenever help is needed. Is there a project that may need more hands? Take the initiative to ask for a role. Your boss will appreciate the extra help. Even if your help is not needed, your boss would at least know you are willing to chip in. This is one of the easiest ways on how to make your boss like you.
5. *Stay out of trouble.* Do not get involved in office politics. Do not gossip. Do not speak ill about other colleagues—be it in your team or otherwise. Not only will you suffer for your own words and actions, your boss will too. Create good working relationships across departments. Another way on how to make your boss like you is to stay out and avoid giving your boss any trouble. When you go to your boss with challenges you face, always bring two to three solutions and state your preferred solution to the challenge you are facing.
6. *Be like a dry sponge.* Soak up the working culture around you. Learn the working styles of your colleagues and how you can find competitive advantage for yourself. Observe how personnel dynamics work in the office—like who can get things done due to their influence. Become a quick learner of everything.
7. *Pick up cues of how your boss works.* Learn, observe and ask how your boss likes things done. The best person to ask is your boss and those closest to him. Learn from other's mistakes when they work with your boss. People will complain when the boss reprimands them, and that is the best time to learn what doesn't go down well with the boss.
8. *No job is a bad job.* People like to pick and choose jobs or projects assigned to them. They choose to believe that some have more value than others. To

a certain extent that is true. But it is also true that bosses know who are the ones who are sincere in helping and uses these opportunities to learn. No assignments are bad at an early level. Every project is an opportunity to learn. Take the assignment from your boss graciously and do your best. It will not go unnoticed.

9. *Don't try to get away with things*. When you make a mistake, come off clean and do not try to cover up. That's one way on how to make your boss like you. Dont try to get away with things also means do not do your work by testing how little effort does it need. Some people are always trying to get work off with the least possible effort and at a passable rate only. Strive for excellence in everything that you do. Let the quality of your work shine. Your boss will know.

10. *Be Early*. If you want to know how to make your boss like you, be punctual. Sometimes this can mean be early at work. Do not turn up for work later than your boss. When you leave for the day, let your boss know you are leaving and ask if anything needs to be attended either that day itself or the next day. Of course, there are many more ways on how you can make your boss like you. These are some of those that can work easily.

Like everything in life, you need to do this sincerely in order for it to work. Remember, you don't have to kiss up or pal around to be liked by your boss. Just be the best employee you can be, listen to your boss's needs, and follow-through. Even if your personalities don't click, he'll have to respect the job you're doing, and that will make your work life pleasant.

MAKING YOUR BOSS LIKE YOU WITHOUT SUCKING UP

There are many things you can do that are completely

legitimate and won't make you look like a suck up. Here are ten simple ways to make your boss like you without sucking up.

1. *Never gossip about your boss.* If you have anything negative to say about your boss, don't talk about it with your coworkers. Instead, wait for work to end and talk with your non-coworker friends about it. It is very likely that anything negative you say about your boss will eventually reach his/her ears. This can make an enemy out of someone in a higher position than you which can severely hurt your career and reputation.
2. *Get to know your boss.* If your office culture allows casual conversation during the day, make an effort to stop by your boss's office and ask how he/she is doing. Ask about their weekend, families, hobbies, or whatever else they might be interested in talking about. Your boss will probably have family photos, vacation photos, and other important items posted on their walls, which makes starting a conversation easier. After learning a little about them and their lives, you can have more conversations with them in the future. Learning more about your boss is something that is free and enjoyable and can benefit you greatly. So take some initiative and get to know your boss a little more.
3. *Ask for advice.* If you have a work or career related problem, ask your boss for advice. Asking for advice will show your boss that you trust him/her and you value his/her opinion. If you act on the advice you get, follow up and tell your boss what happened. Validating your boss's advice will make him/her feel better and will strengthen the relationship you share.
4. *Don't slack off.* Make sure you stay focused at work and don't slack off. Limit the time you spend

chatting with coworkers, snacking, and surfing the internet. Try to keep work in front of you at all times so it at least looks like you are doing something. If your boss gets the impression that you slack off too much, he or she will lose your trust and think you're working less than you might be. When you are not as involved in your work, time will move more slowly, and your day will just seem longer. So stay on task and really wrap yourself in your work.

5. *Maintain a positive attitude.* Maintaining a positive attitude will help boost the moral of your boss and coworkers. Talk about the things that are going well on a project and be optimistic about overcoming the problems you face. No one benefits from or enjoys someone who worries and complains about everything.

6. *Don't be a yes man.* Being a yes man will make your coworkers and boss despise you. A yes man often comes off as insincere and sleazy. Also a boss will never treat a yes man as an equal, which greatly limits future advancement. Being a yes man is bad, but that doesn't mean you should constantly disagree with your boss. Be professional and have the confidence and smarts to agree and disagree with your boss when the time is right.

7. *Keep it professional.* It doesn't hurt to spice things up every now and then at the office, but for the most part, keep it professional. Don't plaster your walls with comics or internet jokes and make sure your attire is always appropriate. Don't be too casual at work because work is supposed to be taken seriously. If you take a more casual approach to work, your boss may think you are uninterested in your career.

8. *Produce results.* Make sure you can produce results on the projects you are working on. If you ever get stuck ask around for help until you are able to complete a given task. This will give you a reputation of being a hard worker and will give you a chance to interact with your coworkers in a positive way.
9. *Be consistent.* Get to a level where you have a good relationship with your boss and stay on course. Be consistent in everything you do to continue building the relationship you have with your boss. If you fizzle out or show signs of change, your boss will likely be turned off by that.
10. *Have good relationships with your coworkers.* Having strong relationships with your coworkers can make a huge difference in how your boss perceives you. If your coworkers love and respect you, it is likely your boss will too. Having strong relationships with your coworkers will also make it easier for you to find help, and delegate tasks. Your boss will see this and give you more responsibility which can lead to future career advancements. Having good relationships with your coworkers will also make your work life more enjoyable.

WORK BEHAVIOUR THAT KEEPS YOUR BOSS HAPPY

If you have proper work behaviour, you will impress your boss. However, you do need to be consistent with these behaviours. There are no results without hard work. That said, each of the behaviour discussed is not difficult to practice. There are many good working attitudes you can put into practice. Of course, the most important thing is to be consistent with it. You can practice just one positive attitude well and it can bring very positive results. However, this does not mean you do not practice the rest. One of the many pressures of being new at work is that people will constantly be watching you. They will see how long you can survive and they will watch your working attitude.

Be Attentive

Learn to be attentive at work. Your behaviour at work should be one of attentiveness. To begin with, you need to be a good listener. Listen to the instructions that are given to you. Make sure you understand what is being said and what is being asked. When you take the wrong instructions you make the unit you are working for inefficient. Attend to details. Make sure every work that you have your hand in is one of excellence. You know the results shine because you paid attention to the details. Never deliver shoddy work. Your shoddy work not just reflects on you but your boss too. When you are attentive at work, your boss will naturally notice you.

Be Bold

Even if you are a junior at work, you need to be bold. Being bold means being able to face your fears. You are new and there are a lot of things that are new to you. You quite naturally fear some of the processes. Sometimes, you may even feel intimidated by some colleagues. In such instances, you need to be bold. There is nothing to fear as long as you know your working attitude is a positive one. This also means you are willing to fail and learn from failure. When you accept this behaviour you are willing to take risks and willing to do new things. Someone who is courageous enough to try new things, willing to fail and learn from failure will catch the boss's attention.

Be Calm

If your personality is quite naturally a calm one, this

working behaviour is easy. If you have a tendency to panic or you have the tendency to be temperamental then you need to work harder. Be calm and composed at all times regardless of the work challenges in front of you. Remember if something tough is for you to tackle, create a plan to solve it. Everything else short of solid action will be inefficient use of your energy. Your bosses want someone who can help to clean the mess. You shouldn't be part of the mess. Remain calm and composed at all times. This behaviour will have your boss take a second look at you. Soon you will become someone he can depend on.

Be Dependable

When you become a competitive advantage for your boss, your boss will like you. He/she will become dependent on you. Strive to become someone your boss can depend. How do you make this work? For starters, be a good listener and be someone your boss can trust. Do not be tempted to get involved in office politics. The best way to stay away from office politics is to shut up. Knowing when to keep your mouth shut should be your work behaviour. Do not add to comments. Do not volunteer answers. When your boss can trust you and you have good working attitude, you will become someone your boss can depend on.

Be Energetic

This work behaviour isn't just about physical energy. It also means mental energy. It also means infectious energy. This means you have a work behaviour that can energise your unit. You are passionate about your work. People like working with you, as you seem to have endless energy. Ever noticed how a person in the office that has energy always gets the better assignments?

That's because their energy is the boss's competitive advantage. You may already posses these work behaviours. Choose one work behaviour that you feel is the easiest to tackle now and work on it.

Be Cooperative

Being cooperative will easily get you well liked. Being cooperative means to know your role well and play that role. So, from the onset make sure you know what your position entails. Sometimes, being cooperative also means taking the initiative to go beyond the call of duty to facilitate your colleague's work.

Have 'Can Do' Attitude

Make sure that your attitude includes a 'can do' attitude. Never give up no matter how tough the task seems. Never say you cannot do this for reason you were never taught how to do it. The cardinal sin being saying, "They never taught me this in college." You may laugh and say the person who said this statement must be stupid. Such statements are common amongst fresh graduates in the working world. If you feel lost, ask. But never say you cannot do it.

Be Careful

Care enough about your work. Strive for excellence in everything that you do. You are measured by the results of your action at work. Do not expect to be successful with your career if you do not care about your own career. Care enough about your career and it will take care of you.

Be Cheerful

Let's face it, no one likes to work with people who sulk, whine and complain the whole day. Be cheerful and energetic at work. It lets your colleagues know that you enjoy what you do. Smile and walk with a spring in your step. A cheerful attitude is an easy attitude to practice at work. Remember to greet people with a sincere smile in the morning. That's a start.

Be Honest

You should make being honest and sincere your working attitude. Be truthful in your dealings. Do not be secretive at work. People do not like others who seem to have a lot to hide. It doesn't build trust, which is a basic ingredient in making sure the team delivers the best results. If you do not know something, say you don't and find how. Ask for the answer. Do not pretend that you know and not deliver. Your working attitude will determine how high you fly in your career. It will also determine how people relate to you. Obviously, the above list of working attitudes isn't exhaustive. It is a start.

WHAT TO DO WHEN YOUR BOSS IN A JERK

As long as you see your boss through your "jerk" filter, your boss will be a jerk. Let that go and see your boss as just your boss. Don't make judgements or put labels on the boss. Realise that your boss just is. Shifting your perspective will help you to begin to shift the energy around how you think and respond to your boss.

One of the most important things one can do is manage the manager. Learn what your boss wants and doesn't want, likes and doesn't like, and how to do the kind of job your boss is looking for. Remember that you do work for the boss and the boss is paying you, so as long as what the boss is asking for is legal, then it is your job no matter how stupid it may seem to you to do what the boss requests. Understand that your boss is not going to change. If change is going to happen, it is going to be up to you. You will have to change the way you interact with your boss. Once you begin to act differently, the boss may respond differently, or not, but it will be up to you to make the change and you will be in control of your own actions and responses. Know that it does not matter if you like your boss. You do not have to be best friends with the boss. You do, however, have to have a professional relationship. That means that you do not complain or gossip about your boss and you get your job done.

Understand that you have a few choices here. You can stay and live with it or you can leave. You can either adapt to the situation or leave the situation. If you feel like the boss has done something illegal, you can always see a lawyer and find out what your rights are. You might also talk to someone in your Human Resource Department or the Equal Employment Opportunity person in your company. The thing to remember is that you are never powerless. Even if all you can do is control your own actions and attitudes, remember you are in control.

Documentation will support you if you ever have to file a complaint. Keep detailed records about the interactions with your boss, the work you are doing, and anything else that may seem important. Documenting what you do just makes good sense. It will also help you at the end of the year when you are trying to remember everything you did. Don't expect your boss to remember; even a great boss won't. They have way too much to do. It is up to you to keep detailed records of how you are contributing to the organisation.

Everyone is someone's difficult person. You may very well have a personality conflict with your boss. Ask yourself honestly how you are contributing to the relationship with your boss. It does take two to dance. Ask yourself how you are making things worse. This can be hard to look at, but can also give you some insight into your own behaviour and how you can remove yourself from the drama. Sometimes, with or without realising it, we are making the situation worse. Step back and see how you might be doing that and stop. This isn't a matter of giving up or letting the other person win. It is a matter of maintaining your sanity.

HOW TO MAKE YOUR BOSS YOUR FRIEND

There is always the possibility of becoming friends with a boss or manager. You will be sharing a great deal of time together and it is quite natural for this to happen. You will learn a lot about each other as you work late or travel together. You may even do things socially out of the office. There is nothing wrong with this as long as you remember that he or she is still your boss and has a lot of control over your career. For this reason, don't tell personal secrets or compromising information to your boss. It will undermine your credibility and effectiveness.

Remember that politics does not mean sucking up to the boss. You will find 'yes' people in every organisation. The world is full of too many suck-ups who tell people exactly what they want to hear. Some managers love to be surrounded by people who tell them they are right even if they aren't. Don't agree just to be agreeable or because of your boss's title. This does you, your boss and your company a great disservice. If you have a better way of doing something or an opposite opinion, present it. Be frank and direct with people. Don't allow yourself to be walked on.

To have a good relationship with a manager or boss, you must communicate what you need and want. Don't say what you will and will not do, but tell your boss the best way for you to get along and work effectively together. A boss can help your career development, but only if he or she knows where you want to go. Tell your boss about your career plans, what you would like to accomplish, and what you need in order to reach those goals. If you need assistance or help, tell him or her. Your boss is a resource and is there to help you. It is not an adversarial relationship. You work in tandem. The better you do, the better your boss looks. It is in his or her best interest to see that you do well.

If your boss is very people-oriented and outgoing, don't sit back and be reserved. Use the language and buzzwords that he or she does. If you do so, he or she will identify more with what you are saying. Find out what buttons to push, and which qualities your boss admires in people. Learn what he or she values in employees. To find out, ask around or ask your boss directly. Your manager will respect the fact that you are taking an interest in learning his or her expectations. You will also know how you will be judged in order to get on the right track. It is best to ask these types of questions early in your tenure with a new manager or boss. To play the game, you have to first know the rules.

MAKING A PRODUCTIVE RELATIONSHIP WITH YOUR BOSS

It is one very significant and important aspect of our working lives, which we need to manage and often forget to, is our relationship with our boss. No matter how difficult and tyrant your boss might be you have to always keep cordial and friendly relations with him because after all he is accountable for you and just as he need your co-operation he is also there to help you out in your difficult times.

You have to remember to work as a team and though at times you may be really mad at him or you may not be agreeable to his plans and ideas but if it is necessary for the benefit of the company you always should stand by you. Never take out your personal indifferences with your boss on the unity and integrity of the company as a whole. And after all your boss might not be a bad person at all. All you have to do is get to know him and you might be amazed to know that he is a gem of a person.

Here are a few tips experts recommend for a harmonious and productive relationship with your boss:

— *Don't try to change your boss if he is difficult on you or if you dislike him.* Instead, try to understand him and his manner of working and make an attempt to adjust accordingly. Find out what aspects of work he is particular about and pay extra attention to those. You can learn many things from your boss and gain from his experience and exposure to work.

— *Try to understand yours boss.* Try to know what he likes best and what he hates. After all he is a human and he will have his strengths and weaknesses. Don't look down on him or focus on his negative aspects. Develop a positive attitude towards him. He might be a great person but probably your negative attitude is keeping you from seeing his good qualities and virtues.

— *Keep him/her informed.* The boss doesn't like to hear about things from other people. Always inform him first whether it is the latest development on your project, an issue in the office or even a personal concern. And never surprise him with new information in public.

— *Include him/her in get together or any team activity.* Make your boss feel like a part of the family, not an outsider. He will appreciate your acceptance and friendly gesture. Always value his opinion.

— *Always give him a helping hand and ask how you can contribute.* Your boss will definitely value an offer which makes his task easier without him have to ask you to help him out. So always ask if you can help in any way to make his current project successful.

— *Make sure you keep your word when you give it.* If you think you wouldn't be able to accomplish something in the given time frame or within the given parameters, provide alternatives. Instead of flatly refusing try "I won't be able to do this by tomorrow but if you give me one more day I can."

— *Try to build a rapport.* Be close to your boss. Get to know him not as a boss but as a person. There is nothing like forging a bond with your boss. Once both of you build an understanding, you will be able to work better and communicate more effectively. But to achieve this goal and developing this will require some effort on your part. You will have to adjust yourself to your bosses needs and moods.

— *Never talk bad about your boss behind his back.* Things have a way of getting around and even people with the best of intentions can accidentally let things slip out of their mouth. In a professional environment, it is best to never crib about your boss. You may have said things in the heat of the moment after a bad experience with your boss, but when your boss hears them, his attitude towards you might just change for the worse. So it is always better to control your emotions and keep them to yourself.

— *Flattery works.* It is a fact that most human beings like to be complimented and appreciated. And a person who receives positive comments from you will generally feel positive about you. But make sure that your flattery is not too insincere.

2

Understanding Your Boss

It is a fact that many people lose jobs most often because they have not been successful in satisfying the demands of their boss. They lose out because of faulty boss relations; because they lack an understanding of boss psychology. By working with your boss you can become free to move ahead and not become lost in the great unknown depths of the business world. Work becomes more pleasant and you become more productive. You gain more satisfaction because you are able to record more achievements. It all becomes possible by using one of your greatest assets—your boss.

A good relationship with your boss is more important for you than it is for them. You have more to lose from a poor relationship than they have. And on top of that, you have only one immediate boss, while they almost certainly have more than just you in their team. So you're going to have to make the running here. Your first step is to get to understand your boss. You need to know how they operate and what is important to them at work. To do this, you need to answer certain questions:

— What does the boss actually do?

— What sort of boss are they?

— What are their strengths and weaknesses?

— How does your boss communicate?

— What motivates your boss?

— What stresses your boss?

You can answer these questions easily with a bit of thought—they're not going to take you weeks of research. Even if you or the boss are new to the job, you can still find out what you don't know with a bit of observation and perhaps a few strategic questions to your colleagues.

UNDERSTANDING BOSS'S OBJECTIVES

Your job is to help the boss achieve their objectives. They probably have wider-ranging objectives than you, and you are responsible for only a part of what they hold responsibility for. For example, they may be responsible for sales throughout the country, while you are responsible only for sales in the south-west region. Or they may manage the entire accounts department, while you deal only with bought ledger. So identify your boss's objectives. For example, their job may be to boost positive PR coverage for the whole organisation, or to ensure a smooth and cost-effective despatch system for all goods sent out to customers. Whatever their precise function, it's likely to be more comprehensive and to have more impact on the organisation than yours. The point of this exercise is two-fold. That is to say, it will help you to understand:

— How much greater your boss's responsibilities are than your own. This helps you to put their relationship with you in perspective. Much as they may want a strong relationship with each of their team members, you may be a much smaller part of their working life than they are of yours.

- The scope you have to be of more value to your boss. While your top priority is to meet the objectives in your job description, the most valuable team members are the ones who can give their boss support wherever it's needed. Without treading on your colleagues' toes, you can still increase your value to your boss by being able to step in when they need support elsewhere, because you understand the priorities and issues for the whole department, not just your own part of it.

Here are a few more questions to ask yourself; the answers will help you to understand your boss's job better, and how you fit into it:

- How many people does your boss manage in addition to you?
- How many people is your boss answerable to, and who are they?
- How much of your boss's time is spent simply managing the department (running team briefings, training, handling staff-related paperwork, communicating, holding interviews and appraisals and so on)?
- How much of your boss's time is spent generating and promoting ideas?
- What sort of decisions does your boss have to take?

By the time you've answered all these questions, you should have a good picture of the tasks and concerns that occupy your boss's attention. You will be able to see that while a good relationship with you will make their life vastly easier, they don't have as much time as you to invest in it, and they have wider concerns than yours.

UNDERSTANDING THE NATURE OF YOUR BOSS

There are lots of different types of boss and, while some

are certainly better than others, many are neither good nor bad, except perhaps in relation to you. We all have our own working style—some of us like detailed work, some hate risk-taking, some are intuitive decision-makers and so on. You need to identify your boss's working style so you can do your best to fit in with it. Here are a few examples of types of working style—your boss may exhibit several of them.

— *Bureaucratic*: This boss sticks to the rules, and likes paperwork. They're not great risk-takers. To keep them happy: you need to put things in writing and stick to the rules yourself. Don't bother putting forward any proposals which involve taking major risks.

— *Laid back:* Results are more important to this boss than dotting i's and crossing t's. So long as things are going well, they won't be too concerned with details. To keep them happy: don't bother them with petty details, just focus on getting the results they want.

— *Consultative*: If you have this kind of boss, they are likely to involve you in decisions, projects and information, and keep you in the loop generally. To keep them happy: don't be secretive around them. They won't necessarily want to be bothered with every detail of what you're up to, but they will want to feel that your general approach is as open as theirs.

— *Non-consultative:* Quite the reverse, this boss never tells you what's going on until they decide that you need to know. While their judgement may often be right (if frustrating), sometimes you need to know more than they realise. To keep them happy: don't ask for information you don't require. If you do need to know something, explain why, so they realise your need to know.

— *Concerned with detail*: This is not necessarily the same as being bureaucratic, although it often goes alongside it. You need to identify your boss's working style so you can do your best to fit in with it. Breathe down your neck most of the time if they can, always wanting to know the nitty-gritty of what you're doing and why. To keep them happy: give them plenty of progress reports and supply all the detail they want. This will make them feel they can trust you.

— *Focused on the big picture*: This boss doesn't want to be hassled with minor detail. They are concerned with objectives and results, and how they are achieved is your concern, not theirs. To keep them happy: don't trouble them with small things—use your initiative. Express ideas and suggestions in terms of the objectives and results that interest this boss.

— *Creative*: Originality and inventiveness are what grab this boss, and they want ideas and creative suggestions from you about everything from how to double sales to a novel approach to the Christmas party. To keep them happy: learn from them—and from other sources such as books—how to exercise your creative mind so you can approach problems and challenges in the same way they do.

— *Logical*: This boss likes all ideas and suggestions to be based on logical reasoning, not on creative leaps of the imagination. Facts and figures should back up every argument. To keep them happy: make sure you have data to justify every proposal or solution you bring to them.

— *Organised*: A tidy desk and a well-kept planner or diary are the hallmarks of this boss. They like plenty of lists, and they always know what their priorities are, both short- and long-term. To keep them happy: look organised yourself. This boss won't believe you can work effectively if your desk is a mess and you're always late for meetings.

- *Unorganised*: This boss may work very effectively, but they don't look it. Papers all over the place, always wondering where they're supposed to be next, and never quite appearing to be on top of the job. To keep them happy: learn to anticipate what they will want, because they won't. Give them plenty of warnings and reminders before deadlines or important meetings, but don't give the impression you're nannying them.
- *Proactive*: New projects get this boss excited, and they're always looking to initiate schemes and ideas. To keep them happy: show enthusiasm for their ideas, and be ready with plenty of your own, geared towards key objectives.
- *Reactive*: This boss spends more time responding to issues and ideas than initiating new ones. So they tend to be more thoughtful and less inclined to take risks. To keep them happy: don't try to get them to launch endless new projects. Instead, concentrate on getting the job done thoroughly and seeing things through to completion. Bosses come in all shapes and sizes, and there's no one perfect type of boss.

UNDERSTAND BOSS'S STRENGTHS AND WEAKNESSES

You need to identify what your boss's strengths and weaknesses are, both in their work style and in the way they handle you and other people. Once you know this, you will have a better idea of where your boss needs support, or where you will need to make allowances. After all, your boss is only human, and none of us is perfect. Your boss has to be allowed a few flaws and weaknesses, and it's up to you to be able to manage them.

Recognising your boss's strengths is also useful. These are areas where you can relax, as well as learn from your boss's example. While strengths are essentially positive for you as well as the boss, some bosses are very sensitive about any criticism—direct or implied—in areas where they feel confident of their abilities. So don't give the impression you're trying to tell your boss how to do something that they already do well.

Here are a few questions to answer, to help you identify your boss's strong and weak points:

— How do you and your team mates feel about your boss? What do you like most and least about them?

— How popular is your boss among colleagues outside the department?

— How well does your boss handle people who make mistakes?

— Is your boss prone to emotional displays? If so, which emotions do they show most often, and are these negative or positive?

— Does your boss get the best from you? If not, how could they get more from you?

— What part of their job would you say your boss was best at?

— What part of the job are they weakest at?

— How close does your boss come to meeting the objectives of the department?

— Is your boss good at making decisions?

— Is your boss supportive of you and the rest of the team?

— How does your boss communicate?

Communication is essential to any manager's job, and it will help you to understand your boss's personal style. In particular, you need to analyse their level of openness, and their ability to put information across.

As far as openness is concerned, consider how readily your boss passes on information to you. Some bosses tell their team everything they can, and others are naturally highly secretive. But most are somewhere between the two, having certain types of information they tend to withhold or pass on, and not others. For example:

— Background information about current projects.

— Information from other departments.

— Information from senior management.

— Confidential information.

— Information about customers.

— Information about competitors.

Many bosses will be very open with some of these categories but not with others.

Once you've identified the areas where your boss is open—and not so open—you can get a picture of what determines their openness. Maybe they don't give information because they don't realise you need it. Or perhaps they're worried they'll get into trouble with management or colleagues. Or maybe they don't trust you to keep confidential information that way. Or perhaps they think you wouldn't understand the implications of certain types of information.

Once you can see the picture, you can start to manage your boss to be more open with you by working on building their trust in you, or by explaining why it would help to have certain information. Some bosses tell their team everything they can, and others are naturally highly secretive. When it actually comes to imparting information, some bosses are very good at it, while others are hopeless at explaining things so they make sense. If your boss falls into this category, you're going to have to do some work yourself to make sure there are no crucial lapses of communication. If you don't understand instructions or briefings, you could be in trouble, and your boss will insist they explained everything clearly to you so it must be your fault.

If your boss is poor at communicating information clearly, the solution is two-fold:

— Keep asking questions until you have the information you need. Don't be afraid to say, "I don't quite understand why this is being handed over to our department". It's far better to say that you don't understand than to keep quiet and then make mistakes later.

— Put your understanding of the information, the brief or the instructions in writing and e-mail it to your boss saying, 'This is just to confirm the brief for the report on the results of the recent PR campaign'. That way, if you've got anything wrong, the onus is on your boss to correct it now before it matters.

HOW TO MOTIVATE YOUR BOSS

All bosses want to see results, but there are plenty of other factors which make them feel more or less motivated during their working day. For instance:

— A convivial working atmosphere.

— A feeling of being in control.

— Challenge.

— A sense of order.

— A relaxed atmosphere.

— Positive attitudes.

— Good relations with other people.

— Competition—perhaps with other organisations, or with their own track record, or with colleagues.

Your boss needs to be motivated to enjoy their job just as you do, and often you can help with this. If they like to be surrounded by enthusiasm, or enjoy feeling that tasks are being carried out methodically, or simply want to have time for a good meal in the middle of the day, you can often provide, or help to accommodate, these things.

KNOW WHAT STRESSES YOUR BOSS

Just as it helps to know what motivates your boss, so it is clearly useful to know what stresses them. The more you can work to reduce their stress levels, the better your relationship with them will be. So compile a list of the things that most get up your boss's nose. Here are some possibilities to get you started:

— Time pressure.

— Pressure from senior management.

— Problems.

— A noisy atmosphere.

— Negativity.

— Not being consulted by team members.

— Being bothered with what they see as petty details.

— Lack of organisation.

— Conflict.

UNDERSTAND THE PRESSURES OF YOUR BOSS

Your work and your mood is affected by your boss, so it stands to reason that they are influenced by their boss—their mood, their attitude, the demands they make. You can't hope to get to grips with your own boss unless you also examine this relationship. You can start by conducting the same kind of analysis of your boss's boss as you have just done for your own.

If you don't know your boss's boss as well as your own, your answers may be a little skimpier, but that's OK —you're at one remove from this boss. You should still be able to get a clear enough picture to understand what pressures your boss is under, and where they are well supported. Having gone through this process, you can flesh out the picture more by analysing a couple more points:

— How good does the relationship between your boss and their boss appear?

— What are the main areas of friction?

Appearances aren't everything, but if the relationship is particularly strong or weak, it will show. If you can identify the main areas of friction, this will indicate where your boss feels most under pressure — when their own views or style are contradicted by the directions that come down to them.

You also need to consider the company culture as a whole. It is very difficult — indeed often impossible — for your boss to operate counter to the prevailing culture. If the organisation is highly competitive, they will have to be competitive to survive. If their boss, senior management and the organisation as a whole has little regard for staff welfare, your boss is going to find it impossible to put staff welfare at the top of their look at your boss's prevailing attitudes in the light of the corporate culture. Every policy or action that requires approval from above will be rejected.

Look at your boss's prevailing attitudes in the light of the corporate culture, and you will often see a pattern. This is not to say that any negative attitudes on your boss's part are blameless — after all, they chose to work in this culture. Nevertheless, attitudes which are backed up by the organisation as a whole are much harder to shift, and you need to recognise this. If your boss does try to break away from the norm, they will put themselves under great pressure, and will need all the support they can get.

LEARN TO INTERACT WITH YOUR BOSS

Now you have consciously considered how your boss works, and what makes them tick, you have the information you need to build a strong working relationship. All this information tells you how they like people to interact with them. For example:

— If you've established that they are a stickler for detail, you'll need to make sure you give them detailed data and progress reports.

— If they hate anything that smacks to them of lack of professionalism, you'll need to make sure you present work neatly, turn up on time and don't criticise the customers in front of them.

— If one of their weak points is a short temper, you'll want to avoid winding them up, and brush up on your skills for handling anger or tantrums.

— If they are motivated by status, show them you respect their seniority, and sell them ideas by concentrating on what a successful outcome would do for their reputation.

— If your boss is easily stressed by time pressure, always deliver work early and do what you can to ease time pressure for them.

— If your boss is poor at communicating background information, learn to ask the right questions and let them know why you're asking.

— If your boss is under pressure from their own boss, they will need a great deal of back-up and support from you to resist it. Don't simply put equal and opposite pressure on them—help them find a solution that keeps everyone happy.

All this should give you a clear picture of why you need to understand your boss in order to build a good relationship with them. The more you know about them, the better you can target your own skills and style to mesh snugly with theirs. And that's the key to managing your boss.

UNDERSTANDING YOUR BOSS'S BODY LANGUAGE

Body language is always a subjective issue and one that needs to be approached carefully. A point that is especially true in the context of your manager or boss. It's never going to be easy understanding your boss. They are, after all, a human being and we all know how unpredictable humans can be.

Your Boss is Human

You might not agree with that statement all the time, especially when they are yelling and screaming like a mad man—but it's a fact. They are human and that means they make human mistakes. They might use the wrong word to give you some feedback—turning a constructive 'You've done well but you might want to look at this for next time' into a 'You've not done well at all have you? , but that doesn't mean they can treat you how they want. It does, however, mean that even the bosses with the best intentions can get it wrong.

Signs like folded arms, detached stares and leaning over a big wooden desk may put you off guard and make you feel more defensive than need be. Your boss may just be making a point in all the wrong ways. It's often worth remembering that your boss feels the highs and lows just like anyone else. The best managers can remain professional and supportive throughout; the worst will make you want to resign on the spot. And then there are the millions of managers in between. So the next time your boss comes towards with their finger in the air, remember that the finger might not be as bad as you think.

Anxiety and Stress

In situations of high anxiety and stress, body language becomes distorted leaving those interpreting it in a state of flux. Those that project it—equally confused. When you are stressed or anxious, particularly in the work place, things can easily get blown out of proportion. You might think your boss is being unfair, aggressive or over bearing. From their point of view, when they are stressed or anxious, your boss may want to smile but their body is telling them to frown. Everything can easily be turned upside down—and when that happens, you enter a whole world of misunderstanding.

Never a Good Thing

If things start going a bit pear shaped at work and everyone is on edge — try to take a moment to remember that the situation may seem a lot different than intended. Your boss maybe looking very angry when, in fact, they are just trying to make sure that things go smoothly. Having said that, stress and anxiety is never an excuse for treating someone with disrespect or harassing someone in an unacceptable way. Whilst you can make allowances when the going gets tough, there is still a line and that line shouldn't be crossed.

There are some great bosses out there who can take the highs and the lows of the business in their stride. They remain professional, courteous and supportive in any situation. Then there are the other managers that you may have had the unfortunate pleasure of dealing with in your career. In any case, there are situations where is worth remembering the fallibility of the human being to upset and annoy other people when they really don't mean to. When you're stressed, anxious or angry than you may come across in an entirely different way to what you intended. And your boss may do the same.

A little bit of understanding can go a long on both sides and the work relationship will be that much better for it. But it must always be said that there is a line to what is acceptable and what isn't. It's great to be understanding but people shouldn't go so far and cross that line.

IMPORTANCE OF COMMUNICATION

Sometimes your boss can seem like they're on another planet. They make no sense and trying to understand them is like dealing with four year old child. A lack of understanding between an employee and their boss can be one of the most frustrating and upsetting parts to a job so it's worth sorting out the issues — early on. Here are a few points on understanding your boss:

— If you don't know what your boss would you to do then ask. It seems a little obvious but a lot of people will just sit there stressing about a task they've been giving by their boss rather than asking. They don't want to seem silly or look like they don't understand.

— If your boss talks at you, in what seems like a foreign language, asking you to complete a piece of work — don't be afraid to turn around and say 'I'm sorry but I don't understand what you mean'. It won't make you look stupid or silly. You will, however, look stupid if you do a piece of work and get it completely wrong. It's always better to ask rather than put in a lot of effort and find out its all wrong.

— Make sure you repeat the task back to your boss. That will give them the confidence that you know what you're doing and give you the confidence to go away and do a great job.

— If you don't know something then be brave enough to say so. People will trust you and will give you more respect if you're willing to admit it when you don't know something, and speak up when you do know something.

— Don't try and fake it because your boss will find out sooner or later. Lying just puts you under more pressure to get it done before they find out.

— You'll look a lot worse if you try to fake it than you would have it you could have just admitted that you didn't know the answer or you hadn't done the work.

— If you put effort into the relationship with your boss then it will pay dividends in your day to day job. It's more than worth it when you consider that you spend more time at work than anywhere else.

TIPS TO MAKE YOURSELF A PART OF YOUR BOSS'S TEAM

Here are few tips to help you plan ahead how to make yourself indispensable to your boss as part of his team; how to eliminate unnecessary daily conflicts that consumes your energy in unproductive activities:

1. You need to change your concept of being a "boss" as well as being "bossed." These are different roles that can be enjoyed "if" well played. It requires understanding on the part of both the boss and the subordinate that one role cannot be effectively played without the other role being diligently

played to complement the other. That are demands for each role, and these demands can only be completed if integration of the other role is accomplished. It is then, a give and take relationship that need to be sustained if we want to create an attractive, motivating work environment.

2. Avoid hostility, harshness, and friction with your boss. Difference in personalities will sure cause some frictions, but these should not be taken personally. They need to be interpreted against the situation that created them. If we believe that there are more than one way to create a mutual understanding and empathy. Uncontrolled perception would always result into misinterpretation of behaviour, resulting in turn into more friction and conflict, which makes the workplace "a fighting arena" of winners and losers.
3. Help your boss become a better manager. This mean "accepting" the other with a belief that regardless of our being different, we still can work together. Personal defects are more felt among friends, but in the workplace these can be accepted as long as they do not influence our performance. Do not try to make your boss look bad before others, especially his superiors. He/she has got more "power" to settle accounts making your life miserable. Learn how to "invest" in your boss by educating him/her without even hinting you do.
4. Develop a daily "game plan" to make it possible to stress positive thoughts, good emotional balance, and be in charge of yourself. You need to "sell" your ideas without being "pushy" or aggressive. Your tool would be "persuasion" not "power". Remember, you cannot impose on your boss. He can.

5. Put your entire group—in addition to your boss—to work for you. Make them feel that your are a valuable asset to the team. This relies mainly on your ability to exert effort to be helpful and cooperating whenever you can. Enhancing your interpersonal skills of communication and negotiation would help become most effective in this area.
6. Have an eye on becoming a boss yourself. Invest in yourself. Do not leave a chance to learn from your mistakes as from your successes.

Your biggest challenge though would be dealing with an insensitive boss. A boss who is too much results oriented. Bosses of that kind are usually inconsiderate to their people's needs. You need here to work winning ways to gain their attention and recognition. Allow enough time and work systematically to develop an interactive relationship with a boss of that kind until you win his/her respect.

3

How to Make Good Relationship with Your Boss

Your boss is key to your on-the-job satisfaction and to your future success in the organisation and perhaps even beyond. If there ever were a relationship for you to invest in, this is it. The number one thing is to observe the company culture and your supervisor closely during your first few weeks. Keep your opinions to yourself until you understand the company culture well and know what people will look upon with favour and what they'll look upon with disdain. Even something as simple as asking intelligent questions will make a difference in how your boss perceives you as an employee. It's always better to clarify than to charge off and go completely in the wrong direction.

Some bosses are very hands-on, keeping close tabs on you throughout your workday. Others may talk to you once a week or less often and send you on your way to do your job. Whatever your supervisor's style, typically it's up to you to establish and maintain the lines of communication between the two of you. Using either e-mail or the occasional stop-by-the-office visit, make sure you keep your boss informed with the answers to these questions:

— What are you working on?

— What have you finished, and what are the results?

— What can you help your supervisor with?

Effective managers take time and effort to manage not only their relationships with their subordinates but also those with their bosses. Managing your team as a leader is as important as managing your boss.

Some people behave as if their bosses are not very dependent on them. They fail to see how much the boss needs their help and cooperation to do his/her job effectively. These people refuse to acknowledge that the boss can be severely hurt by their actions and needs cooperation, dependability and honestly from them.

A manager's immediate boss can play a critical role in linking the manager to the rest of the organisation, making sure that the manager's priorities are consistent with organisational needs and in securing the resources the managers needs to perform well.

Managing the boss requires that you gain an understanding of the boss and his/her own context, as well as your own situation. At a minimum you need to appreciate your boss's goals and pressures as well as his or her strengths and weaknesses. Such as what are the boss's organisational and personal goals and objectives? What are the pressures? What are your boss's long suits and blind spots? What is his preferred style of working? Does she/he like to get information through memos, formal meetings or phone calls? Does s/he thrive on conflict or try to minimise it? Without this information, a manager is flying blind when dealing with the boss and unnecessary conflicts, misunderstandings and problems are inevitable.

The boss is only one half of the relationship. You are the other half, as well as the part you have more direct control over. Developing an effective working relationship requires that you know your own strengths, weaknesses and personal style. One cannot change the basic personality of oneself or one's boss. But one can become more aware of what it is about you that impedes or facilitates working with your boss and take actions to be more effective.

Gaining self-awareness about oneself and acting on it are difficult but not impossible, but this could be managed by reflecting on past experiences. Although a superior subordinate relationship is one of mutual dependence, it is also one in which the subordinate is typically more dependent on the boss than the other way round.

Counter-dependence (when the subordinate acts on his or her negative feelings, in subtle or nonverbal ways, the boss sometimes does become the enemy) and over-dependence (managers who swallow their own anger and behave in a very compliant fashion when the boss makes what they know is a poor decision) lead managers to hold unrealistic views of what a boss is.

DEVELOPING AND MANAGING A GOOD RELATIONSHIP

With a clear understanding of your boss and yourself, you can usually establish a way of working together that fits both of you, that is characterised by unambiguous mutual expectations. A good working relationship with a boss accommodates differences in work style. Subordinates can adjust their styles in response to their bosses' preferred method of receiving information. Peter Drucker divides bosses into "listeners" and "readers". Some bosses like to get information in a report so that they can study it others like it better when information is presented to them so they can ask questions. So the implications are obvious if your boss is a listener you brief him/her in person then follow up with a memo. If your boss is a reader you convert important items in a memo and then discuss them.

Other adjustments can be made according to a boss's decision-making style. Some bosses prefer to be involved in decisions and problems as they arise; these are high involvement managers who like to keep their hands on the pulse of the operations. Usually their needs are best satisfied if you touch base with them on an on going basis. Other bosses prefer to delegate-they do not want to be involved. They expect you to come to them with major problems and inform them about any important changes. Creating a compatible relationship also involves drawing on each other's strengths and making up for each other's weaknesses.

Expectations

The subordinate who passively assumes that she/he knows what the boss expects is in for trouble. Some superiors spell out their expectations very explicitly but most do not. Though many organisations have systems that provide a basis for communicating expectations these systems never work perfectly. Also between these formal reviews expectations invariably change.

Ultimately the burden falls on the subordinate to find out what the boss's expectations are. They can be both broad (what problems the boss wishes to be briefed about and when) as well as very specific when a particular project should be completed and what kind of information the boss needs in the interim.

If a boss is vague and not explicit it maybe difficult to get information out of him but effective managers find ways to do that. Some managers will draft a detailed memo and follow up with a face-to-face discussion. Others will deal with an in explicit boss by initiating an ongoing series of informal discussions about "good management" and "our objectives". Still others find useful information more indirectly through those who used to work for the boss and through formal planning systems in which the boss makes commitments to his or own superior. Which approach you choose would depend on your understanding of your boss's style.

Developing a workable set of mutual expectations also requires you to communicate your own expectations to the boss, find out if they are realistic and influence the boss to accept the ones that are important to you. Being able to influence the boss to value your expectations can be particularly important if the boss is an over achiever. Such a boss will often set unrealistically high standards that need to be brought into line with reality.

Managing Information Flow

How much information a boss needs about what a subordinate is doing will vary significantly depending on the boss's style, the situation he or she is in and the confidence the boss has in the subordinate. But it is not uncommon for a boss to need more information than the subordinate would naturally supply. Effective managers recognise that they probably underestimate what their bosses need to know and make sure they find ways to keep them informed through processes that fit their styles.

Managing the flow of information upward is particularly difficult if the boss does not like to hear about problems. Nevertheless for the good of the organisation the boss and the subordinate, a superior needs to hear about failures as well as successes. Some subordinates deal with the good-news-only boss by finding indirect ways such as a management information system. Others see to it that potential problems are communicated immediately.

Dependability and Honesty

Few things are more disabling to a boss than a subordinate on whom he cannot depend, whose work he cannot trust. No one is intentionally undependable. A commitment to an optimistic delivery date may please a superior in the short term but become a source of displeasure if not honoured.

It's difficult for a boss to rely on a subordinate who frequently misses deadlines. Dishonestly is another issue. It's almost impossible for bosses to work effectively if they cannot rely on a fairly accurate reading from their subordinates. Because it undermines credibility, dishonestly is perhaps the most troubling trait a subordinate can have. Without a basic level of trust a boss feels compelled to check all of a subordinates decisions, which makes it difficult to delegate.

Effective Use of Time and Resources

The boss has limited time, energy and influence. Every request a subordinate makes uses some of these resources so it's wise to draw on these resources selectively. Many managers use up their boss's time over relatively trivial issues. No doubt some subordinates will resent that on top of all their other duties they also need to take time and energy to manage their relationships with their bosses. Such managers fail to realise the importance of this activity and how it can simplify their jobs by eliminating severe problems. Effective managers recognise that this part of their work is legitimate and know the need to establish and manage relationships with everyone on whom they can depend including their boss.

IMPACTS OF GOOD WORKING RELATIONSHIP

The relationship a manager has with his boss is of

fundamental importance to the ability to perform well within the role. The relationship needs to be managed and has to be a conscious act and not simply a case of being pleasant or getting along well together. What is being managed is the relationship—not the individual.

A good working relationship between you and your boss should enable you to develop your skills, knowledge and career and combine:

— Fairness.

— Mutual respect.

— Trust and rapport.

— Openness and honesty in communication.

Managing your boss is about constructing a relationship of trust, respect and support. It means acknowledging who is boss but maintaining the freedom to do the best for the organisation, the team and yourself. The key word is "manage"; implying an on-going process and not a one-off activity.

Positive workplace relations rely on three skills:

1. Having a good understanding of the person (people) that you have relations with.
2. Seeking first to understand others and then to be understood.
3. Using positive communication strategies.

Having a good understanding of others helps us adjust our behaviour to be able to get along well with them, thereby building good rapport. Understanding someone's uniqueness can be accomplished by having an awareness that people have different personality behavioural styles. Each of these styles has distinct, predictable and observable behaviour patterns. Once you understand these personality styles, you will have the ability to get along with almost anyone.

Once you learn about the characteristics of each dominant personality style, you can quickly learn to read the person with whom you are dealing, and make minor adjustments to your own behaviour to relate better with that person.

Since the basic need of a human being is the need to be understood, listening is more important than talking when in conversation with someone. Real empathic listening means that you are doing more than hearing someone's words. It means that you seek to understand what they are saying and will provide feedback once you have heard what they are telling you. This ensures that you understand what has been said and that the person speaking feels like they have been understood.

When we feel that we have been understood, we are likely to feel better about the relationship, resulting in more productive relations. The next time you have an opportunity to communicate with someone, tell him or her that you would like to listen to them first, giving you the opportunity to gain a good understanding of what they are communicating to you. Once you offer feedback to what you have heard, and the speaker feels that they have been understood, you will be in a good position to begin the final step of building strong and positive relations.

Positive communication is productive because it fosters some of the key fundamentals of successful workplace relations including, trust, honesty, integrity, nurturing, productivity, and satisfaction. At this point in your communication with someone you would have an understanding of their personality style, and have empathically listened to them making them feel that they have been understood. Forming positive messages is more attainable when you can 'begin with the end in mind', meaning you have an idea in your mind of what the positive relationship would look like. Once you have this goal of the communication in mind you are in a better opportunity to attain that goal. Strategies recommended for positive relations include making the other person feel good about themselves and their contribution. People feel good about their employment when they are recognised in a positive and genuine way. Therefore, positive communication can start with a genuine compliment and carry forward from there.

Remain professional at all times. The number one way to avoid problems with other people at work is maintain a professional decorum every day. This does not mean that you hold yourself aloof from your co-workers, but rather that you make it clear by your behaviour that you are first and foremost a professional, and that you take your job very seriously. Be friendly, but not overly personal with your co-workers. Show people that you are there to accomplish your job.

Set an example. People who get in trouble at work are generally those who engage in workplace gossip and complain endlessly with co-workers. You have established yourself as a professional, now you need to set an example of professional behaviour. Avoid getting involved in petty discussions and if you find yourself in the situation, try to steer the conversation into a more positive direction. You can be friendly with people and even engage in friendly conversations, but try not to get entrenched in other people's problems. This can suck up valuable work time and keep you from accomplishing your goals.

Guard your privacy. Over time, you will become close to certain people with whom you work. There's no avoiding that. From time to time, you will be invited to lunch, company functions and even a night out after work. Socialising with co-workers is a great way to foster teamwork and an important part of business life. But while you socialise, you also need to remember to keep a balance between your private and your work life.

Be careful whom you trust. Certainly there will be people in whom you feel comfortable confiding your problems, but be careful whom you trust. The most unwitting comment could be used against you at some point in time. There are almost always people at work who are looking for ways to get ahead, and by exposing a weakness, you might be giving them an edge.

Set clear boundaries. If an office relationship appears to be turning a bit more personal than you would like, it is important that you make your boundaries clear. This is not easy, and must be done with tact and care. Be sure that what you perceive is, in fact, correct. If a co-worker clearly comes on to you, make sure they know in no uncertain terms that this is not acceptable to you. If this behaviour continues, you may be forced to take more serious action.

Advantages

There are great advantages to managing your relationship with your boss:

- It's the most important working relationship you have.
- It creates a productive and communicative working relationship.
- It ensures each of you knows what is possible and feasible, *en route* to achieving the results that matter to you both.
- A good working relationship improves your self-esteem.

Disadvantages

There are no disadvantages to managing the relationship,

but disadvantages to not doing so. Fail to manage the relationship with your boss and it: can create a manipulative relationship where office politics or personal style dominates the way you and your boss work together:

— Can hinder open communication.

— Can make you lose self-esteem.

— Can make problems or conflict harder to solve.

Action Checklist

1. *Communicate properly* on time, in adequate detail and regularly; make sure formal communication works, but also ensure you simply talk and compare notes from time to time. Prevention is better than cure, and effective communication prevents a lot of misunderstandings and breakdowns in relationships.
2. *Identify any blockages.* Examine your current relationship with your boss. Identify where the blockages to a good working relationship lie—perhaps you have trouble communicating, or find it hard to express your own opinions or have discussions about workload. Identify what triggers these problems. Also think about parts of the relationship that work well. Build upon these and work on cutting problems in other areas.
3. *Identify your boss's leadership style.* It is important to be able to recognise the way, or ways, that your boss typically acts or behaves towards you. The following are typical leadership styles: bureaucratic, charismatic, dictatorial, consultative, laissez-faire, abdictatorial. A specific style or mix of them will require different approaches from you. Think too about your boss's 'thinking' style. It's no surprise

that we get on well with some people but others rub you up the wrong way. Try to figure out if your boss is one for the minutiae, for the 'big picture', reactive or proactive, likes or hates change, is a right-brain or left-brain boss.

4. *Identify your boss's key objectives and values.* Think about what is important to your boss and work hard on these areas. The two main areas to pay attention to are:

   — his/her objectives—what, in the eyes of your manager, are the key objectives and what support can you give towards achieving them?

   — what personal values your boss holds dear-for instance customer care. Work on supporting these values and don't do things that are contrary to them. Be wary, however, of evidently self-interested values, such as personal status.

5. *Clarify boundaries of responsibility.* Sort out with your boss exactly what decisions you can make

   — after discussion with your boss

   — on your own but reporting to your boss afterwards

   — on your own with no need to report.

   Lack of clarity can be a major source of conflict and friction.

6. *Tackle the simple issues.* Look through the problems you have identified and decide which are the simple issues to solve. Can small administrative problems be solved by introducing a simple new system? Discuss minor sensitivities with your boss and try to reach a compromise. But don't relay your mastery of trivia when your boss would expect you to deal with them as routine—don't waste time

reporting unimportant successes. Work overload is often a common cause of conflict. Don't take on work you can't manage—be honest but remember your manager's objectives and always suggest an alternative solution. Don't underestimate yourself or your point of view. If you don't have faith in your ability to do a good job and develop in your role, your boss certainly won't.

7. *Tackle longer term issues with assertiveness.* Some blockages can't be removed overnight. Concentrate on building up a stronger relationship with your boss. This means being assertive but not aggressive. Express your point of view, respect your boss's opinions and work to find mutually acceptable solutions to existing problems. This will improve the value of your relationship and help you to handle difficult situations more effectively in the future. Don't loop the system by going over your boss's head—however attractive this may seem. If you feel blocked , tackle the issues directly to avoid creating other problems later.
8. *Focus on loyalty and support.* Concentrate on supporting the weak spots in your boss's make up without making it too obvious you are doing so. Find out what parts of the business they enjoy and are good at, and those she/he doesn't like doing or perhaps doesn't have the skills to deal with. Make yourself indispensable. Show you are keen to learn skills which complement your boss's skills. Win their trust by achieving things they value.
9. *Think about how other people see you.* People can assume a lot about your abilities from the way you look or the way you present yourself. They may think a scruffy, sullen looking person is disorganised, bad at their job and generally

unreliable. Look smart. Smile and act positive. Celebrate your successes. Make sure your manager knows when you have done well and that your success is theirs too.

10. *Seize on opportunities*. Keep your eye on the big picture and not just the task in hand. Don't use an overload of work as an excuse to avoid activities such as attending conferences or meeting senior directors. Weigh up the short-term disbenefits against the potential longer-term value for the organisation. Think about what these opportunities do for your development and what you could learn.
11. *Communicate your agenda*. There's no need to be abrasive, but a modicum of repetition may be useful in making sure that your agenda gets heard. This may relate to specific projects or on-going work but think about the bigger picture too. What do you want to learn? Where do you want your career to go? Instead of always playing your boss's tune, develop joint objectives.
12. *Review issues and actions, and plan future development*. Appraise issues which are important to you and discuss them with your manager. They are actually important to them too, because if you fail, your boss fails. Discuss problems before they get out of hand and have some ideas for solutions ready to talk through.
13. *When relationships are genuinely difficult*. Most of this checklist holds good if you have a boss who is a fairly reasonable human being. Sometimes you may be faced with a boss from hell. Three of the worst types of boss can be the bully, the sexually harassing boss, and the glory-stealing boss. It is not easy to deal with any of these although there is some protection from employment law to draw on

with the first two. Take a look at the further reading for ways of dealing with the glory—stealer-there are techniques involving keeping records, collecting evidence and bypassing your boss.

14. *Nip conflict in the bud.* If conflict breaks out between you and your boss-handle it. Don't run away or tackle anger with anger.
15. *Review the relationship.* Sit down from time to time and ask "How are we doing?" Focus on the relationship so that you both know where things stand, and can work to improve and maintain the underlying relationship between you. If a conflict-or a particularly successful joint approach-has occurred, use it as a vehicle for reviewing the relationship and work out what to do again in future and what to do differently next time.

DOS AND DONT'S FOR MANAGING YOUR BOSS

Dos

— Make the time and take the trouble to talk to each other.

— Form an alliance-understand your manager's objectives and values.

— Remind your boss that you are on the same side.

— Learn to support the weaker areas of your manager's style.

— Be wary of gimmicks like encouraging your boss to think your idea was his/hers.

— Appraise and review your current work, future goals and the relationship.

Don't

— Be passive-always doing what your manager wants and not putting forward your own viewpoint.

— Be aggressive-fighting fire with fire rarely works.

— Go over your boss's head if you can avoid it.

— Ignore problems and avoid discussing them.

4

How to Impress Your Boss

Neglecting to impress the boss could be hazardous to your career. Most bosses are astute in recognising that special something that makes employees stand out from the crowd. The best way to impress the boss is to become a low maintenance employee. That entails showing up to work on time. Next stay out of the gossip column. There is nothing worse that getting caught up in the gossip that takes place on the job.

It's common for high achievers to struggle with a tendency to over commit. Their desire to accomplish great things can cloud their ability to set reasonable limits. Unfortunately, good intentions can backfire. Many superstars' reputations have burned out like meteors because they started dropping important balls. Employees who consistently deliver on their promises impress bosses. Reminding employees of unfulfilled commitments causes resentment from bosses--not respect.

When given an assignment, don't make assumptions. For instance, if asked to prepare a report, "when you get a chance," it would be wise to request a specific target date. If you are unclear on what your boss expects from you--find out! Knowing the right questions to ask--and when to ask them--is a sign of a true professional. And it can save you from many unnecessary communication breakdowns. Bosses appreciate employees with enough concern (and common sense) to get the facts so that expectations are met. It shows you have good foresight and planning skills--two impressive qualities.

Excuse makers are a dime a dozen, and they rarely move ahead. Admitting weaknesses takes courage and self-awareness--two admirable qualities. If you don't know, say so. If you make a mistake, admit it. Then, take the important step of cleaning it up! Employees who refuse to accept accountability are very frustrating to bosses. People generally won't kick you when you are down. We all make mistakes, and it's refreshing to hear someone own up to theirs. If you stubbornly deny responsibility for your mistakes, however, you can count on a rude awakening--and a displeased boss.

Professional dress is a sensitive topic. Nobody likes to think they dress inappropriately, but in reality this shortcoming certainly does holds people back. Dress like the position you wish to attain is a good rule of thumb. Sure, it seems superficial. You may protest that people should not judge a book by its cover. In principle, you may be right. But human nature and principal do not always match. If you lack the judgment to dress professionally, don't be surprised when people assume you have deficiencies in other areas also. To impress the boss, dress like one yourself.

Bosses are ambitious people who recognise and admire that same quality in others. Ambition requires ample confidence to stick your neck out occasionally and take a risk. Bosses cherish talented employees who demonstrate their desire for excellence in a variety of ways and on a regular basis.

Always make yourself available for the new projects that need to be done. Be a person that takes the initiative to get things done on time. Make sure you meet your deadlines. Over deliver. If you say you can have it done in a week get it done in two or three days. Just be sure you have given yourself adequate time.

Lead the next team meeting with the boss present and relay to the team your vision for the organisation or a particular project that you are working on. Let the team know if everyone comes together with the team concept you are more likely to get things done because of the synergy that will take place. Synergy means the whole is greater than the sum of the individual parts or better yet 1+1 = 4. Also let the boss know that you intend to hold a meeting with the boss not present. In the meeting let everyone know that you expect them to give their all to meet the goals of the department and emphasise how it will make the boss look good if the goals and objectives are met.

Have confidence and poise. When you are confident in your ability to complete a task or in your own individual skills this will impress the boss. They will consider you as someone who has a future with the company and will likely recommend you for promotion should one come available.

Always have good ideas. Keep a lot of good ideas in your pipeline and let your boss know what they are. Your ideas should include how to save time, money and how to motivate and develop people. It might be a good idea to have some ideas about how to capture market share.

Share your best demonstrated practices. If you have a process of procedure that works to perfection 80% of the time it is a good idea to share it with your coworkers. This will increase the effectiveness and efficiency of everyone on the team and in turn make your boss look 100% better. Give your boss credit for the things he has done to help you develop as an employee and a person.

All these things done together will serve to impress your boss and ensure you have a successful career with your organisation.

HOW TO IMPRESS YOUR MUCH OLDER BOSS

Get a raise and the respect of a much older boss by following the steps below:

- *Show interest and enthusiasm.* A boss is interested in workers that make an effort to understand the work and that show the desire to get the work done.
- *Actively listen.* This means asking questions when things are not clear and repeating back what has been said in your own words to be sure you have understood what has been said. This is particularly helpful if the boss does not use words or terms that are familiar.
- *Do not fake interest.* Most people can detect false interest. The idea is not to try to make the boss feel adored about everything he or she says.
- *Determine what is important to the boss.* Most supervisors have particular things that are very important to them such as neatness, tardiness etc. Find out what is important to your boss and do what counts.
- *Be on time.* Many supervisors judge the attitude of an employee by when they show up for work. Ten to fifteen minutes early can really help your image. Remember most supervisors work overtime and do not get paid for it.
- *Be dependable.* Be careful what you promise and always deliver on what you promise.
- *Do not make excuses.* Take responsibility for your part of whatever is wrong. Then explain what else happened if it is even necessary to tell what else happened.

— *Do not complain.* If there are safety, legal or harassment issues then you must speak up. If your work is not illegal or immoral or unsafe then just do the job. No work is always pleasant or easy. Otherwise why would anyone want to pay someone to do it?

— *Treat your boss like a customer.* The reason you are getting paid and keeping your job is often how well you treat you boss. Your boss does not have to be your friend or personally close in any way but he or she should be treated with respect and helpfulness.

— *Don't expect your boss to understand you.* Your older boss may very well not understand your words or terms or understand what is important to a person your age. Stick to using common words that are used to conduct business at a bank or store. Do not try to use words from his or her youth. This effort can easily be misunderstood. Your bosses job is to work for his or her boss. Help them do that job well and you will be well treated.

— *Do not object change before carefully considering the outcome.* The positive results of change, whether to the organisation or to you personally may not be obvious. Talk your concerns out to your boss. Be positive.

— *Do not be misunderstood.* It is easy to have your friendliness mis-interpretted as social interest. This particularly true if you are not the same sex as your boss. Make sure your boss knows that you are working for an income not a social contact. If you are really attracted to your boss, change jobs. If your boss is really attracted to you change jobs.

— *Do not talk about your bosses age.* You are both there to do a job. Comments about "back then" or "when you were young" etc. can easily be misunderstood.

HOW TO SUCK UP TO YOUR BOSS

Initiative pays. So does subservience. If you want to get in good with the big cheese, you've gotta be prepared to kiss some ass. These instructions will get you on the path to becoming a first class suck-up.

— Find out where he or she takes his or her dry cleaning and pretend you live nearby. That way you can always say, "Hey, big guy/girl, I can drop something off at the cleaners if you want."

— Station yourself in the parking lot before and after work. If you're the first and last person your manager sees every day, you'll seep into his or her subconscious.

— Eavesdrop on their conversations, then feed him or her back their ideas as if they were your own. He or she will think you can read his or her mind.

— Offer to help him/her with some paperwork and do it somewhat often, because if it seems like you are willing to help him/her with the dullest of things, he or she will know that you are someone they can count on.

HOW TO TELL YOUR BOSS THAT HE IS MISTAKEN

When your boss' mistake is going to create a problem for your employer, a customer or another department, it is appropriate for you to prevent the problem. You must be careful not to offend or anger your boss when doing so.

— Be certain your boss actually made a mistake.

— Identify the problem that this mistake will cause in business operations.

— Ask your boss if he/she would like to be informed if you discovered that something he/she did might cause a problem in the business.

— If your boss does not welcome the information, ask, "When I see that problems are about to occur in other areas of our business, how would you like me to handle the situation?" Follow those directions.

If your boss is receptive to learning about her/his mistake, explain it in this way:

— Tell your boss you are proud to work with someone who does the right thing—good bosses need and deserve acknowledgement from the employees who report to them.

— Focus on the effect the mistake will have on the business, not on your boss' shortcomings, to show your initiative in trying to follow good business practices.

— Talk to your boss privately and in person, if possible, or by phone if a one-on-one meeting is not possible.

— Do not approach your boss if you intend only to show that he/she was wrong. This will damage your relationship. We're all human and we all make mistakes.

— If your boss is intentionally making mistakes because he/she is stealing time or assets from the business, make sure her/his boss is not also involved in the scam before anonymously informing upper management of the issue.

— If corruption is wide spread in your organisation, consider finding another employer where the work practices are consistent with your integrity.

HOW TO DISAGREE WITH YOUR BOSS

This really applies to disagreeing for specific valid reasons in almost all situations. It requires that the person you are disagreeing with be willing to engage you in discussion on the topic, and assumes they are not completely closed minded.

- Start out by having at least one specific, valid and provable reason why you know this idea won't work.
- Begin asking the person questions to help you understand their views on the idea you disagree with.
- When they answer, follow up with another question which leads in the direction of your reason for disagreeing.
- Liberal use of 'we' is helpful, but don't overdo it. If something is clearly your opinion use 'I'.
- Be willing to consider the possibility that you are wrong.
- The goal is to make the person reach the same conclusion on their own. Don't expect this to happen immediately—give it some time.
- Doesn't matter what, never try to prove that you are better than the boss.
- If an idea doens't work tell them you'd like to try a different approach. Don't make it seem as if they are wrong. Just add to the problem solving arsenal.
- Simply tell them you disagree. Have a conversation and see where it goes. You may not know of experiences your boss has had or they may not understand your thinking process. Adults and professionals disagree everyday. Some of the best ideas come from brainstorming and disagreements.
- Remember, ultimately they are the boss. If you are specifically told to do or not do something a certain way then you should respect the authority. You never know where they are getting their cues or

what demands upper management could be making of them.

WHAT THE EMPLOYER WILL BE LOOKING FOR

Once you have secured yourself the job of your dreams you want to ensure that you keep it. Your new employer will have invested considerable time and money hiring you and it is up to you to prove to them that they made the right decision in doing so. There are numerous qualities that an employer will expect from you regardless of whether you are the office junior or departmental manager.

Punctuality

Start as you mean to go on by arriving into the office ten minutes early this will give you time to exchange pleasantries with your colleagues, perhaps get yourself a coffee and settle yourself before the day begins. If you arrive at work bang on time, or late you will probably have been rushing, you may be out of breath, and will certainly not be in a relaxed state conducive with beginning good work. Punctuality shows your employer that you are organised and can manage your time efficiently, these are important qualities to convey, especially if you have your sights set on rapid promotion.

Dress

Unfortunately we do judge books by their covers and first impressions usually are the ones the last longest, clients will make a judgement of your company's success, competence, and mentality based upon your office building, the décor and unavoidably the appearance of the staff. Many new companies are abandoning formal wear in the office and are opting for jeans and T-shirt's.

Every work place has its own dress code and you should be aware early on what that code is. It is an unspoken rule within the banking and finance industries that business suits should be worn every day. Conversely in new media and IT jobs you can get away with rolling out of bed and stumbling into work in your *pajama*as long as you are able to write wicked source code and are happy the boss won't object. Whatever their policy you should adhere to it if you want to fit in within the company. If it is formal dress it is recommended for men to wear a suit, their shirt should be is clean and ironed, they should wear sensible smart shoes and a tie void of cartoon characters. Women arguably have more flexibility and can wear a suit, a smart skirt or trousers, shirt or any smart top. It is a fallacy that women get ahead by showing off cleavage, excess boob exposure is unadvisable as it can wreak havoc with male productivity and you might catch a chill.

Competency

You are hired to do a job, and regardless of whatever else goes on in your office you have to do the job that you are paid to do. Not only that but you should take pride in your work, do not rush tasks, manage your time efficiently and make a good job. Once you are in your job do not rest upon your laurels, you should continue to develop new skills and your employer will be particularly impressed if you cultivate expertise that are useable within your job and are of benefit to the company. For example learn how to make websites, use databases, speak french etc.

Sociability

Make an effort to be friendly and approachable, you will not stay in your job long if you do not fit in with the rest of the team. Even if you have a personality clash with another colleague you should try to get around it, and don't bitch about other employees. Your employer will want to see that you have fitted in well. It is just as important is to make acquaintances with your counterparts in other companies. If you are attending an outside training course or an industry exhibition be friendly and social towards the other delegates. Even if that chap from across the pond does have a statically charged suit that attracts little bits of tissue you should still take his business card, you never know, he may prove to be excellent contact.

Positive Attitude

It is important to be enthusiastic about your work, with a good positive attitude. Punctuality and a high quality of output are indicative of enthusiasm, your employer will pick up upon these things. Be forthcoming with ideas, you should be looking towards the future, scoping out other possible sources of revenue. Come up with more efficient ways of doing things within the office, just because something has been done a particular way in the past that does not mean it is the best way of doing it. After you have been in your new position for about a month look back at the job description that you applied for.

IMPRESS YOUR BOSS WITH YOUR COMMUNICATION SKILL

Everyday, we have many people we need to communicate with: our partner, our child's teacher, our friends and the cashier at the store, among others. However, there is one person who your communication with will affect your bottom line. That person is your boss. So how do you communicate effectively with this person who exercises direct control over your paycheck? Here are ten tips that will help you feel more confident next time you encounter your boss.

1. *Watch how the boss communicates with you.* Does the boss prefer to use e-mail, phone or direct contact with employees? Follow her example. If she prefers to e-mail you about small issues, then follow suit. If important issues, such as those involving large amounts of money are usually discussed in person, then do likewise. Do be aware that all e-mails that you send should be composed using correct spelling and grammar. You are always making an impression, even when she can't see your face and well-groomed hair!
2. *Make sure that your timing is good.* If you need to communicate that the mail carrier has already stopped by today, then it is probably okay to do so when your boss has one foot out the door on her way to a meeting. If you need to discuss a performance review, make sure that it takes place at a time when your boss is in a pleasant mood and is not overly rushed.
3. *Be prepared.* Whether it is in a large meeting or a simple one-on-one conversation, make sure that your communication is accurate, and if necessary, backed up by the appropriate documentation. You don't want to inadvertently give incorrect off-the-cuff information. If you are not sure if your information is accurate, it is best not to say anything, or to say that you will get back to her at a specific time with the necessary information.
4. *Consider the boss's perspective.* It is good in any circumstance to consider the other person's perspective. In the case of your boss, she is more concerned with the company's bottom line than with your need to repair your car. So when you are asking for a raise, for example, make sure that you are communicating what you contribute to the company, not your own financial insecurities.

5. *Look at how the most effective office players communicate with the boss.* Do they do so informally, or do they make appointments? If you observe that your boss enjoys making conversation by the water cooler about the latest in digital camera technology, then by all means join in. If they make appointments with the secretary to speak to the boss, then it is a good idea for you to do the same.
6. *Be aware of your body language.* Standing with your head down communicates a lack of confidence. Holding your arms crossed in front of your body demonstrates a lack of openness. Putting your hands on your hips can seem aggressive. Hold your body in a relaxed manner, while maintaining eye contact. Try resting one hand on a desk, putting a hand in your pocket, or using your hands to take notes.
7. *Maintain control of the conversation.* When communicating with your boss, it is not a good idea to show too much emotion, unless it is enthusiasm or conviction. If you hear your boss making statements that you find upsetting, listen and nod your head. Keep calm. When there is a break in the conversation, quietly make your point. Be sure not to raise your voice or interrupt, as both of these actions give the impression that you are not in control of your emotions.
8. *Find out about your boss.* The more common interests you have with someone, the easier communication becomes. Find out if your boss has children the same age as yours, if she likes soccer, is involved in community organisations that you have an interest in; in short, try to find some common ground. When you find yourself in casual conversation with your boss, listen. Everyone enjoys talking about themselves and their interests.

9. *Focus on the positive.* There are many negative aspects to any job. When communicating with your boss, be sure to focus on the positive aspects. This is true even if you are holding a meeting to address an issue that is potentially loaded with negativity. Accentuating the positive tends to put your boss more at ease. Above all, never react to any statements in a hostile manner. While you are certainly entitled to hostile feelings, allowing hostility to come out during a conversation with your boss will never serve your best interests.
10. *Ask questions.* Don't assume that your boss will think that you are unintelligent if you need clarification on an issue. You might need to repeat back instructions to your boss to ensure that you understand correctly what her expectations are. This is an excellent way to avoid awkward communications in the future.

Communicating with your boss may be tricky at times, but if you keep your cool and follow these basic tenets of workplace communication, then you will be at your most effective, and success will follow.

Communicating with Aggressive Boss

It is tough having to deal with someone who abuses you and even more so when the person has extra authoritative power than you. If the verbal and other forms of mental abuse begin to get really serious and even approach physical abuse, then the issue can become legal. People are trying to pass legislation in an American state that disallows workplace abuse. However, unfortunately just about all laws do not take into account verbal workplace conflict so you've got to learn how to handle bullies by yourself for your own happiness and well-being.

Most people who lack the communication skills to deal with a bad boss either:

— Endure the bullying and intimidation in fear thinking their job is at risk if they address their boss about the problem.

— Face their boss about the problem but do so incorrectly. It's quite common for the problem to then intensify.

The absolute last thing you want to do when being abused by anyone is accept the abuse. You have got to stick up for yourself in an assertive manner otherwise your confidence, happiness, and in this situation, your work will suffer. People who receive aggressive behaviour that is not correctly handled have been known to develop serious physical problems such as strokes, heart attacks, suicide, migraines, escalated stress levels, insomnia, and terrifying nightmares. One person who will remain anonymous often dreamt her boss pointing a gun at employees so they would complete their work.

The first listed reaction to a bullying boss is a passive response. You forgo your own person needs while your boss happily tramples over you. The most common reason for accepting intimidation from others is the fear of repercussions if you stick up for yourself. In a work situation and especially with someone who has authoritative power, you probably do not defend yourself in fear of losing your job.

These passive people forgo their own needs, are dominated by others, and live in massive amounts of frustration as their anger is bottled up inside. They do not have the effective communication skills to address the problem thinking they must accept what happens and live with the intimidation hoping the abusive person stops bullying.

People may become aggressive for several reasons:

— They were abused by their parents at an early age and placed under emotional trauma.

— They are mentally ill. I'm not referring to a jokingly mental illness but someone who has a serious mental illness such as schizophrenia or a personality disorder.

— They think the only way to stop someone else's abusive behaviour is to abuse them back.

— The aggression is a release of anger often caused from responding passively like the first situation. This type of behaviour is otherwise known as passive-aggressive behaviour where the person is frequently passive but randomly explodes their frustration and anger onto others. After the occasional and often unexpected outburst, the person sinks back to his/her passive behaviour.

— The person is experiencing high pressure creating stress and then aggression. This type of aggressive behaviour is common in work environments.

— An aggressive boss maybe trying to prove his toughness, control, discipline, or results-focus to superiors through his/her behaviour.

While aggression in the workplace may create the necessary level of productivity, it is strongly related to a high turnover rate said to be an average of 1.5 years and other commitment problems such as increased days off and loss of passion in the employee towards work. It can create unproductive employees as they "hide" by staying under the radar seeking to comply yet they do nothing that stands out that could potentially bring them attention.

The aggressive communication being exchanged between two people becomes a loss for them both.

Depending on the situation, occasional aggressive behaviour can be definitely welcomed. In order for the aggressive behaviour to be successful it must be expressed appropriately and constructively. You could even say this constructive type of aggression is like assertive communication which must be your goal if you are to not respond passively like the first situation and aggressively like the second situation.

There are several assertive communication techniques you can use to stop the bullying, stop your fear, build your self-confidence, and actually create a nice working relationship with your boss. This is the power of assertive skills.

Before approaching your boss about the problem, ask yourself "What can I change in my behaviour to solve the aggression?" What you are doing is owning your behaviour and not blaming your boss for what you have control over. It creates personal responsibility within you and helps prevent you from blaming your problems on your boss. Sometimes analysing yourself and solving the problem may actually stop the aggression.

You need to be calm but at the same time responsive. Once you do this first step, you will almost completely remove your aggressive communication which can also help reduce your boss' aggressive communication. Fire needs some sort of fuel to stay alight and what you are doing by being calm but responsive is you are removing psychological fuel from your boss' aggressive fire. Being calm isn't enough as it can show that you're ignoring your boss. Only being calm and not responsive hurts in showing empathy and diffusing the boss's emotions. You do not want to ignore an angry boss!

Have the right mindset of resolving the problem at hand. When faced with a difficult person it is easy to want to be only right. Acknowledge that you may need to comprise yourself to progress forward with this problem. Drop your pride and be the first one to step forward towards problem resolution.

Now that you've learned these techniques it's time to approach your boss. You need to find the best time to address your boss. Do not try and solve this problem in a high emotional situation. You may need to wait till the end of the day or even end of the week until you think you can approach your boss.

What you are doing by asking for their point of view first, you are able to see things through their perception which may give you a whole new side to the story. It will help you understand and even help your boss understand why he is aggressive. Your boss will begin to feel understood by you when you actively listen which can lead to a tonne of great things such as him feeling your empathy, knowing you care, having less intense emotions, and be more willing to change. By practising good listening skills you are using the secret of persuasion.

After your boss has made suggestions, you can then give your ideas to solve the problem. Keep calm and stay focused on resolving the problem. Ask for your boss's feedback as you suggest ideas. You are making it a joint solution which will give both of you a greater total level of satisfaction.

As you are talking, take note of the positive points your boss does show in his behaviour and compliment him on these. You are attempting to keep the conversation positive as solving a problem can seem negative even though it is actually good that you are trying to remove the problem!

Using these techniques to communicate assertively will reduce your boss' aggressive behaviour. You will no longer have an unproductive and unhappy working relationship. You'll develop a more productive and possibly joyful working relationship for your own good and your organisation's good. Who would have thought you could have an enjoyable relationship with an aggressive boss.

GETTING ALONG WITH YOUR BOSS

To get along with a boss it is important to understand his/her personality and individual style and have the ability to adapt your behaviour to ensure a positive relationship. Developing good human relationship skills is especially important once you enter the world of work. Understanding your boss's unique personality can make your job as an intern much easier as well as more rewarding and a better learning experience.

It's important for interns and new employees to be able to work independently as well as part of a team. If you are someone who needs direction before completing a task, you will want a boss who likes to maintain a "hands on" approach when supervising others. On the other hand, if you absolutely hate having someone standing over your shoulder and watching you, you will probably be more comfortable with a supervisor who supervises from a distance.

Bosses seek individuals who are self-motivated, energised, and who exhibit a go-getter attitude that gets the work done right and completed on time. It is your job to fit in with the management style and understand how the office operates. By providing your boss with a feeling of confidence in your decision-making skills, you will create an atmosphere of trust and respect and ultimately better working relationships with co-workers and supervisors.

Learning how your boss wants you to communicate and handle problems can make your life as an intern much easier. Bosses are human beings who have their own way of dealing with problems and generating solutions.

Taking the time to learn your supervisor's management style, will go a long way to making your life as an intern much easier. Notice your bosses mode of communication. Does he/she communicate with staff mainly through e-mail and written communications or does he/she prefer face to face discussions?

By maintaining your cool in the heat of an argument, you will exhibit self-restraint and provide an opportunity for you to cool off and think things over prior to speaking. Taking the time to understand a problem will provide an opportunity to replace negative emotions by settling down and reacting professionally.

Every office has its own culture and set of rules, and failure to follow them can be disastrous. Some common 'don'ts' when working in an office:

— Not paying attention to the start and finish hours for the office.

— Starting late and leaving early are definitely not good things.

— Not adhering to the dress code, formal or informal. Establish yourself before you try expressing yourself through your appearance.

— Failure to complete work on time. This can be very upsetting to an employer.

— Letting someone else tell the boss you made a mistake. Be sure that you're the one that tells the boss you have made a mistake. Take responsibility for your own actions.

— Not getting along with other office staff. It pays to be nice.

— Letting your boss know that you're smarter than he/she is. Remember, your job is to make your boss look good, and you can learn something from any boss. Lose the attitude and do what you need to do.

— Not asking for help if you're having problems. Bosses love resourceful workers, but if you're having problems and need help, ask! Don't wait till the problem is out of control.

For almost anyone entering the workforce, dealing with strained relations and difficult personalities is unavoidable. Living and working in a social world requires that from time to time we will have to interact with people that simply rub us the wrong way. Perhaps the most difficult of these strained relationships is the one that occurs between an employee and their boss. While all relationships in a workplace have the opportunity to create problems, the relationships between an employee and their boss may be the most volatile; as well as most threatening to job satisfaction.

The relationship between boss and employee is often characterised by power differentials and expectations. To many people, their boss represents a source of conflict and hostility in the workplace. While this may not be true for everyone, the majority of people in the workforce will have at least one incident in which they disagree with their manager. While most disagreements are healthy, some can explode into battles that cost us advancement, jobs, and even friends. Because of the inevitability of this conflict, it is important to develop the skills to prevent and cope with any disagreement that may arise between you and your boss. By simply keeping a few things in mind throughout the work day, employees can decrease the likelihood of conflict and increase the opportunity to achieve a more satisfying work environment.

Stress Management Techniques

Despite our best efforts to prevent conflict, it is likely that at some point you and your boss will have a disagreement that cannot be communicated through. This may be due to differences in personalities, pressure from upper-management, work related stress, or one of you simply having a bad day. When the incident occurs it is important to remember that despite personal feelings or views, your boss is still a person with power over you and butting heads with them can have serious consequences. Therefore, in order to avoid being reprimanded or even fired, it is important to have a number of stress management techniques at your disposal in order to keep you cool.

Most of these techniques are very simple and can be utilised daily at work. The most important part of these techniques is being able to recognise your stress when it begins to build. One way to alleviate stress is simply counting to 10. When you begin to feel overly stressed, simply count from 1 to 10 very slowly while taking deep, cleansing breaths. By taking this extra 10 seconds to calm yourself, you should find yourself more prepared to deal with conflicts with your boss.

Another important technique for managing your stress is truly utilising your breaks during the day. Many people take their breaks but spend the time worrying about what will happen when they return. Your lunch time and breaks should be a personal moment to recollect yourself and relax. By festering on the events of the day, we overshadow the point of having a break and add undue stress to our day.

Respecting the Chain

No one likes to be disrespected, and your boss is no different. It is very important to keep that in mind when you have an issue or problem that you feel deserves immediate attention. As your manager, your boss has a responsibility to not only ensure that you are doing your job, but also to ensure for your safety and well-being. This means that any issues pertaining to you should be taken up with your immediate manager.

In some cases, you may want to speed up the process by skipping your boss and going directly to an upper manager. While this may seem helpful, it will likely cause hostility between you and your boss. By bypassing them in the chain of command, you have disrespected their authority and may have made them appear foolish to their boss. While your immediate needs may have been met, the boss you regularly deal with now feels betrayed, foolish, and even hostile towards you; a situation which can cause trouble in the future. For this reason, it is usually best to speak to your boss first about any problems you have, even those that pertain to his behaviour. If, after addressing these issues with your boss, you still feel these issues have not been addressed, then it may be appropriate to seek a higher supervisor.

Another issue which can damage your relationship with your manager is that of interoffice gossip. When we feel upset or unappreciated by our boss it is often difficult to hide. It may be even more difficult to keep these feelings from coworkers who share our feelings. While it may feel helpful and therapeutic to talk about these problems with our coworkers, if they have not been identified to your boss, then these conversations amount to nothing more than useless gossip. It is more helpful to keep your issues between you and your manager. By minimising the amount of interoffice gossip, you show respect for your boss and improve your work relationship.

Maintaining a positive relationship with your boss is very important to achieving a satisfying work environment. This positive relationship can be the key to a happier workday, a more fulfilling career, and even more opportunities for advancement. By communicating clearly our own needs and expectations, establishing stress management techniques, and showing respect for the business chain of command we improve our office relationships and decrease the likelihood of conflict in the workplace. With these tools, we can help to decrease office hostility and keep the peace in the world of manager and employee.

Coping with in a Hard Office Environment

Have you ever thought about your own attitude at work? Perhaps that is the reason why people do not like you. For many of us it is easy to look at others and blame them instead of ourselves. After all, we are human. How many of us like to admit our own mistakes.

When something doesn't go the way it is supposed to at work, "Oh, so-and-so didn't do this and that." Often times you forget your own roles that you did not perform. Your attitude is looking at other's fault first before you point the accusing finger at yourself.

Perhaps when you realise that people at work do not like you, then it is time to look at your own attitude. Have the wisdom and will power to know that you can make a positive change. It doesn't mean that you are weak. It doesn't mean that you are a lesser person. It just means that you can improve yourself. When you improve yourself, you increase the chances of career success. Indeed, not just career success but personal success too!

There are people whom the harder you try to please them; they do not reciprocate in kind. In fact, they treat you worse. You may be good to them but they do not return your kindness. You smile at them; they frown back. Nothing seems right. You could be speaking softly to them but they seem to raise their voices at you. You think to yourself, they have a bad attitude at work.

When you are able to detach yourself from it, you begin to see a clearer picture. Think about your attitude at work. Are you being sincere with your words and deeds? Can people feel your sincerity? Do you do things joyfully without expectations from others? Look within yourself and improve your attitude at work.

These tough people that you face at work are your "teachers" on your attitude. They are teaching you to introspect. You may actually conclude that there is nothing wrong with you. So be it. Then continue to do the things that you do once you are convinced that your attitude at work is correct. Eventually they will see the light, so to speak. But if you sincerely do it and look within yourself, your thoughts, attitude and actions—maybe you will discover things that you can improve. Then your attitude at work can improve and people may slowly treat you better. Sure, attitude problems at work are tough to solve. They are tough to solve, not impossible. Sometimes, maybe it is better to start with ourselves.

Some time in your career you will come across having to work with people you don't like. So, how do you work with people you don't like? Admittedly, it is a huge challenge for many people. Even for me personally. I still grapple with the issue. But it is a fact of working life, no matter how much we do not like it, these interactions are crucial to get work done.

Many newbies and veterans alike are caught asking this question day-in and day-out at work—how do you work with people you don't like? Do you force yourself to do it? Pretend we like them? What else can you do besides being pretentious? Do you really leave your values at home when you go to work?

The answer is—no, you do not have to. Of course the remedy may not be easy. It will entail you having to step out of your ego for a while to see what is truly happening and to give you clarity of the situation. That stepping out of your own ego is the toughest to do. But I assure you, is a worthwhile step. Personally, when I am able to do it, it feels like a huge stone is lifted off my heart. How to work with people you don't like? Try the following steps.

— *Engage.* Engage them is one way. To engage in this case means to communicate with them. Step out of your own ego no matter how difficult it is to get yourself to sincerely talk to them. You may be pleasantly surprised that the other person wants to talk. To engage also means not to hold any grudges against the other person. Face the issue with the other party and discuss whatever challenges you may have candidly. Say what you mean and mean what you say politely. You can be stern but do not be rude. Be there to want to solve the challenges you are facing with the person. The important thing about how to work with people you don't like is to be sincere about it. When you are sincere, you are seeking a win-win situation. You are manipulative when you are seeking a win-lose situation. Think about this when you engage this person. Being sincere is also a transfer of feelings. Which means you want the other person to know that you genuinely want to settle any animosity you have with each other. Build a reputation for yourself as someone who tries to work things out with others when things seem rough. That way it helps you in the long run too.

— *Enlighten them and yourself.* Perhaps one reason you do not like them is because you do not understand them. And because you do not understand them everything seems strange and whatever they do doesn't seem right. When you do not understand people you tend to find excuses not to accept the way they do things. Then all these negativity feeds on each other and the animosity grows. If you are able to step out of your ego for a while, you will find that you are able to talk to the person better. When there is new information we evaluate situations differently. Think about this, when you allow the person to communicate something to you without you putting up all the fences and wall, then you start to listen. This new information enlightens you. There is a chance you may decide to react differently.

To let people we don't like, whom we work with to enlighten us is tough. For us to enlighten them takes a lot of effort. That is needless to say. But if you sincerely seek a solution to the challenge then the way you approach how to work with people you don't like will be significantly different. Seek to allow them to get to know you personally. The information and new knowledge about you may enlighten them about you. It gives them insight into who you are, why you do the things you do and the way you do it. When people understand you more, there is a better chance they will begin to like you. Of course, there is no guarantee it will work. At the very least there is a chance. Get to know them on a more personal level too. As much as we allow people to know us, we must learn about them. Enlighten yourself about them. What makes them tick, what is it that you do that disturbs them or even irritates them. Perhaps with this piece of information you may start to know how to work with people you don't like.

5

How to Manage Your Boss

It is just as important to manage your relationship with your boss as it is to manage subordinates, products, markets, and technologies, argue these authors. If the relationship is rocky, neither managers nor their bosses can do their jobs effectively; the responsibility for the relationship should not and cannot rest entirely with the boss.

To many the phrase *managing your boss* may sound unusual or suspicious. Because of the traditional top-down emphasis in organisations, it is not obvious why you need to manage relationships upward-unless, of course, you would do so for personal or political reasons. But in using the expression managing your boss, we are not referring to political manoeuvring or apple-polishing. Rather, we are using the term to mean the process of consciously working with your superior to obtain the best possible results for you, your boss, and the company.

Studies suggest that effective managers take time and effort to manage not only relationships with their subordinates but also those with their bosses. These studies show as well that this aspect of management, essential though it is to survival and advancement, is sometimes ignored by otherwise talented and aggressive managers. Indeed, some managers who actively and effectively supervise subordinates, products, markets, and technologies, nevertheless assume an almost passively reactive stance vis-a-vis their bosses. Such a stance practically always hurts these managers and their companies. If you doubt the importance of managing your relationship with your boss or how difficult it is to do so effectively, consider for a moment the following sad but telling story:

Ram Manohar was an acknowledged manufacturing genius in his industry and, by any profitability standard, a very effective executive. His strengths propelled him into the position office president of manufacturing for the second-largest and most profitable company in its industry. Ram was not, however, a good manager of people. He knew this, as did others in his company and his industry. Recognising this weakness, the president made sure that those who reported to Ram were good at working with people and could compensate for his limitations. The arrangement worked well. Two years later, Philip Jacob was promoted into a position reporting to Ram. In keeping with the previous pattern, the president selected Jacob because he had an excellent track record and a reputation for being good with people. In making that selection, however, the president neglected to notice that, in his rapid rise through the organisation, Jacob himself had never reported to anyone who was poor at managing subordinates. Jacob had always had good-to-excellent bosses. He had never been forced to manage a relationship with a difficult boss. In retrospect, Jacob admits he had never thought that managing his boss was a part of his job.

Fourteen months after he started working for Ram, Jacob was fired. During that same quarter, the company reported a net loss for the first time in seven years. Many of those who were close to these events say that they don't really understand what happened. This much is known, however: while the company was bringing out a major new product—a process that required its sales, engineering, and manufacturing groups to coordinate their decisions very carefully—a whole series of misunderstandings and bad feelings developed between Ram and Jacob.

For example, Jacob claims Ram was aware of and had accepted Jacob's decision to use a new type of machinery to make the new product; Ram swears he did not. Furthermore, Ram claims he made it clear to Jacob that introduction of the product was too important to the company in the short run to take any major risks.

As a result of such misunderstandings, planning went awry: a new manufacturing plant was built that could not produce the new product designed by engineering, in the volume desired by sales, at a cost agreed on by the executive committee. Ram blamed Jacob for the mistake. Jacob blamed Ram.

Of course, one could argue that the problem here was caused by Ram's inability to manage his subordinates. But one can make just as strong a case that the problem was related to Jacob's inability to manage his boss. Remember, Ram was not having difficulty with any other subordinates. Moreover, given the personal price paid by Jacob (being fired and having his reputation within the industry severely tarnished), there was little consolation in saying the problem was that Ram was poor at managing subordinates. Everyone already knew that.

We believe that the situation could have turned out differently had Jacob been more adept at understanding Ram and at managing his relationship with him. In this case, an inability to manage upward was unusually costly. The company lost 2 crores to 5 crores, and Jacob's career was, at least temporarily, disrupted. Many less costly cases like this probably occur regularly in all major corporations, and the cumulative effect can be very destructive.

BOSS-SUBORDINATE RELATION

People often dismiss stories like the one we just related as being merely cases of personality conflict. Because two people can on occasion be psychologically or temperamentally incapable of working together, this can be an apt description. But more often, we have found, a personality conflict is only a part of the problem—sometimes a very small part.

Jacob did not just have a different personality from Ram, he also made or had unrealistic assumptions and expectations about the very nature of boss-subordinate relationships. Specifically, he did not recognise that his relationship to Ram involved mutual dependence between two fallible human beings. Failing to recognise this, a manager typically either avoids trying to manage his or her relationship with a boss or manages it ineffectively.

Some people behave as if their bosses were not very dependent on them. They fail to see how much the boss needs their help and cooperation to do his or her job effectively. These people refuse to acknowledge that the boss can be severely hurt by their actions and needs cooperation, dependability, and honesty from them.

Some see themselves as not very dependent on their bosses. They gloss over how much help and information they need from the boss in order to perform their own jobs well. This superficial view is particularly damaging when a manager's job and decisions affect other parts of the organisation, as in Jacob's situation. A manager's immediate boss can play a critical role in linking the manager to the rest of the organisation, in making sure the manager's priorities are consistent with organisational needs, and in securing the resources the manager needs to perform well. Yet some managers need to see themselves as practically self-sufficient, as not needing the critical information and resources a boss can supply.

Many managers, like Jacob, assume that the boss will magically know what information or help their subordinates need and provide it to them. Certainly, some bosses do an excellent job of caring for their subordinates in this way, but for a manager to expect that from all bosses is dangerously unrealistic.

A more reasonable expectation for managers to have is that modest help will be forthcoming. After all, bosses are only human. Most really effective managers accept this fact and assume primary responsibility for their own careers and development. They make a point of seeking the information and help they need to do a job instead of waiting for their bosses to provide it. It seems to us that managing a situation of mutual dependence among fallible human beings requires the following:

— You must have a good understanding of the other person and yourself, especially regarding strengths, weaknesses, work styles, and needs.

— You must use this information to develop and manage a healthy working relationship—one that is compatible with both persons' work styles assets, is characterised by mutual expectations, and meets the most critical needs of the other person. And that is essentially what we have found highly effective managers doing.

RULES TO MANAGE YOUR BOSS

The relationship with your boss is probably the most important relationship you have at work. Boss management can stimulate better performance, improve your working life, job satisfaction, and workload. Give your boss a hand and reap the rewards. Some important rules to manage your boss are described below:

1. *Decisions.* If you do not want a 'no' or procrastination, give him/her a hand. Your boss has other subordinates, other decisions to make. Thus, his best bet, if he is pressed for a decision, will be to say no. No, it is too risky; no, we do not have enough evidence; no, it is the wrong timing; no, it is off strategy.

— To avoid the 'no' that will ruin your and your team's enthusiasm, give him a hand;

— Remind him of where you left it last time you met;

— Remind him of the objective rather than rushing to the 'what' and 'how';

— Remind him of past problems encountered because a decision was not made;

— Quickly summarise the options considered, your criteria for selecting one option — the one you are presenting;

— Tell him what you expect from him: simply to inform, to decide jointly, to share the risk, to add one criterion, to re-examine the option;

— Focus on the points where you need him help;

— Be prepared with facts/data for potential disagreements. Help him out with graphics and visuals so that the situation is grasped faster;

— After your meeting, summarise for him the decision in writing to make sure of the understanding;

— And finally, once a decision has been made, your way, him way or no way, do not criticise it externally. You have become the best defender; the best ambassador of what was decided.

2. *Manage his time.* You may represent only 1 per cent of his problems, don't make it as if it is 100 per cent. Yes, you have preoccupations, problems to solve and issues to tackle. However, while your time is entirely devoted to them, do not expect your boss's time to be also.

   — The more simple the problem or issue at hand is, the less time you should have his spend on it: prepare, summarise, and synthesise information and options. Do not confuse your more frequent problems with the most important ones.

   — Book his for several meetings in advance. Nothing is more frustrating than to have to wait days, weeks or months for that extra new meeting needed in order to finalise a decision or a project.

3. *An opinion.* If you ask for his opinion, he will always have one.

   Rare are the bosses who, when asked for their advice or their decision, will use the psychological ping-pong approach of returning the question to the person who asked. And their opinion may not always be that of a genius or a visionary. However, once given, the opinion becomes a constraint: was it an order? So, if you don't want your boss's opinion to thwart your achievements, to slow the speed of decision-making, or cloud the viewpoint, then don't ask for it. Best of all, don't ask if you don't need his opinion.

   — *Choose the right moment to avoid procrastination*: not only save his time by focusing on big issues, but choose the right moment to do so. If you present an issue at the wrong moment, the chances are he will procrastinate.

— *Prepare for your meeting*: first because the advantage is to the one who is prepared, second because the preparation helps you reduce the time taken to come to the central issue.

— *Show the forest before the trees in a discussion:* if you want to avoid spending a lot of time on going back to basics before he is at full speed with you, start with the basics yourself. Remind him of the objective, where you stand today, and what you want his opinion on.

4. *Information.* It is not data. Turn grapes into wine: you are supposed to analyse the results of a market survey, and not be the mailman who passes the thick document full of statistics to your boss. So be selective; be visual; group the data; bring out what is essential. Data overload creates stress, which in turn can create denial, rejection, and numbness. As a manager, you are paid to collect the grapes (data), and turn them into wine, i.e. useful information.

— *Don't give him only the bad news:* give him also the good news. If you keep bringing only bad news, little by little you become the bad news yourself. Don't minimise good news, because you want to focus on the problems. By doing that you contribute to creating a bad atmosphere.

— *Make sure he does not get the information from others too often:* sometimes by being shy about what we should give or because we think it is not relevant, we don't feed our boss with key elements. However, other people could do it before you.

— And then you need to justify yourself; you may need to modify incorrect information. The trade off is between too little information leading to starvation, frustration, and/or restlessness vs too much information leading to overload.

— *Participate in and contribute to his informal network:* every manager, hopefully, does not rely solely for managing on formal information given in internal documents and reports. Some people use internal informal networks. Some others also have an informal outside network of experts, friends, business connections that help them shape their vision of the world and how to act. You have yours; your boss has too. Why not volunteer part of yours, so that you do not always have to react and be defensive about information fed by people you do not necessarily think are the best sources?

4. *Problems*. Don't just come with problems, come also with solutions.

   Good bosses hate two kinds of behaviour. The courtesan who always comes to tell you how great you are and the pyromaniac/fireman who comes to tell you "There is a huge problem" and then says "but don't worry, I will solve it!" There is also a third kind, the monkey transferor. He has a problem and he puts it on your shoulders, rather than bringing a solution or at least some options. Problems usually have several aspects. It is usually a gap between an objective and the result; there are options to close the gap; there is a choice of one option to be made; key tasks, dates, people and resources needed must be defined.

   On which of those steps in problem solving do you want your boss's input? Just be clear on what input you want rather than come with the stressful — "I have a problem..." and throw the monkey.

5. *Assumptions.* Do not assume he knows as much as you do, but assume he can understand; so educate him. Please help, you are the expert. You spend all of your time and that of your team on the issue. You live with data, pressure points and levers; your boss does not. He does not know more than you do.

   Most senior executives are even dangerous when they get involved in making micro-decisions, as their point of reference is often not the current one but rather the situation they knew when they were junior managers.

   If you need his perspective, it is because it is broader; he has a better sense for interrelationships with other parts of the organisation. You have two options.

   — You inundate him with technical stuff he does not understand, hoping that the amount of technical jargon will knock him down and force him to agree with you. It may work, but it may become a barrier in communication leading to lack of trust.

   — You educate him by simplifying, using easy to understand language, feeding him with articles, examples, best practices, summaries that help him see a perspective. By creating understanding, you relieve tensions; create trust that can lead to better decision-making.

6. *Delegations. Constantly test the waters.* It is not always easy to define ex ante what is delegated to a person. Some companies prefer to use the principle of subsidiary rather than the principle of delegation: the principle of subsidiary stipulates

that you can do everything except the following list, whereas in the principle of delegation you stipulate, "you cannot do anything except..."

Whichever is used, there will always be some doubt whether you have or do not have the delegation. You have two options: either you play it safe by always asking your boss's opinion. This can lead to paralysis, bottlenecks and your own demise, as your boss will think you are unable to take responsibility. Or you assume too much, take decisions and learn after the fact that it was not yours to decide. In between, there is the 'test the waters' strategy especially for things or areas, domains or steps that are unprecedented.

7. *Promises*. Do not promise what you cannot deliver, and avoid surprises, trust is at stake.

   Trust does not develop overnight and depends a lot on the predictability of the other person: what he says and does, how often he is living up to or not living up to his statements. In the same way, you will not fully trust your boss if he changes his mind too often or says things contrary to what you were told the last time. You also want to avoid being seen as unreliable by not delivering on what you promise or surprising his with bad news without forewarning.

   Do not promise dates for finishing projects you cannot handle. If you see that too much is asked of you, sit down and re-discuss priorities before proceeding, rather than becoming yourself a bottleneck. Involve your boss in the process, so it becomes a common priority.

   Avoid bad surprises. If your job is to be in charge of a particular area, then it is also to be in charge of bad results and improving them.

Involve your boss in discussing and evaluating the risks, agreeing on key lead indicators that you will both share, so that neither you nor he will be surprised. For instance, whereas sales are not a good lead indicator, future orders or bookings can be. Cash in the bank is not, whereas good cash flow three months in advance is.

8. *Trust. Don't be sloppy in your documentation. It undermines trust.* By making the assumption that he will check what we write or say anyway, and that he will make changes, we sometimes tend to be sloppy in our writing. Tables are not finished, text is not re-read, places we are going to are not visited beforehand, spelling is not checked, and information is missing.

By not finalising your facts, arguments, memos, spelling, supporting documents, etc., you can be sure some things will get changed, mistakes corrected. And soon you will be asked to show more facts and figures, and you will see more changes, more amendments. Soon all the delegation you had will be gone.

The quality of management may be rapidly declining in today's corporate world, but the foot soldiers of the workplace can do a lot to help—and enhance their job satisfaction in the process. No disrespect intended, but it appears that lousy management has reached epidemic proportions in the Information Technology industry. Bad bosses can suck the motivation, creativity, enthusiasm, productivity and health right out of decent people trying to do a good job and earn an honest wage.

Bosses have a lot to put up with—like you for instance! And they have to deal with their own set of very challenging pressures and priorities—conflicting organisational objectives, peer relations, functional challenges, their own bosses, etc.

So it's no wonder they often get distracted from:

— Assisting you in prioritising your work;

— Validating your assumptions;

— Providing you with missing information;

— Offering meaningful feedback;

— Connecting you with the rest of the organisation;

— Making sure you're on the right track before it's too late;

— Helping you align the necessary organisational resources.

It's all this potential, then, that makes managing your relationship with your boss perhaps the single most important ingredient in determining your ultimate success.

Consciously working with your superior to obtain the best possible results for you, your boss and the company is a definite Winning Strategy. But how does this work, exactly? One way is to help your boss see that you are looking at issues from his or her perspective—not just from your own. So if you boss is saying no to your killer idea because there are insufficient funds, don't just grouse. Ask your boss what's needed to move forward and how you can help.

If it's an explainable variance memo that's needed, then write one. If the project is seen as too big for some reason, start smaller. If the project is considered too small to have sufficient impact, show how you can ramp up its scale. Whatever the boss' concerns, address them—meaningfully and quickly. Because by solving the boss' concerns, you subtly influence him or her to work more on yours.

Another key is in improving how to complain. Most complaints are caused by broken commitments, stated or otherwise. Therefore, when making a complaint, it's essential that you are able to:

— Clearly and crisply state your complaint and its impact without getting defensive or aggressive.

— Specify the real or implied commitment that was broken.

— Articulate how the responsible person can resolve your concern, being as specific as possible.

— Ask for their commitment to follow through as agreed.

If your complaint is properly addressed, be sure to say, "Thank you." If it's not, say, "Thank you for trying. Now what else can we do about this problem?" And remember, by basing your complaints on broken commitments, you're maximising your impact and minimising everyone's discomfort.

You can also use this commitment-based approach to keep your bosses in line on an ongoing basis. Routinely:

— Ask your boss to make specific commitments to you—no matter how small.

— Remind your boss that he or he is making a commitment to you.

— Follow up when your boss ignores or forgets that commitment by reminding him or her of the broken commitment and requesting an apology.

— Do all of this with a professional, respectful and responsible tone

It's just a fact of life that "bosses will be bosses." You can lessen the probability that your boss will make bad decisions that affect you and increase the probability of your job satisfaction by effectively managing your boss/employee relationship. It takes a little practice, but it's definitely worth the effort.

HOW TO COACH BOSS

The relationship you have with your boss is very important on both a professional and a personal level. It can have a significant influence on your day-to-day job satisfaction as well as your long-term career success.

The relationship is also important to your boss who is counting on you, and your colleagues, to satisfy customers, meet deadlines and achieve objectives. But keeping this relationship healthy and productive is not about 'managing' your boss: it's about understanding them, and you, and then choosing to behave in a way that gets the best results for you, your boss and the organisation.

Only by understanding your mutual needs, styles, expectations, strengths and weaknesses can you develop a relationship that works for both of you. In any relationship what you say and do influences the other person. You can't change your boss but you can control your own behaviour. It's important, therefore, to understand what you do that either helps or hinders the relationship. Here are some actions you can take to make the relationship work. Take responsibility for your own career and personal development

— *Ask for feedback throughout the year—don't just wait for performance reviews.* Learn how to evaluate your own performance—what are you doing well; what do you need to improve on.

— *Take responsibility for performance reviews.* Be aware that not all bosses are good at holding review meetings so help by being as positive as you can be, even if you don't like some of the criticism you may receive.

— *Discuss mutual expectations openly.* Find out what your boss's expectations are and share your own. Tell your boss what development and support you need. Don't assume they'll automatically know. Use your boss's time well and develop good timing yourself. Your boss's time is limited so make good use of it, don't waste it. Find out if your boss is a lark (good first thing in the morning) or an owl (better later in the day) and choose your moment to raise issues.

— *Have a 'no surprises' policy.* Communicate bad news immediately. There's nothing worse for your boss than being called to task by his/her boss about something they know nothing about.

— *Identify your boss's preferred working style.* How do they like to receive information—face-to-face, in writing, by e-mail? How much do they like to be involved in decisions? How organised are they—can they cope with a little chaos? How comfortable are they with risk taking? How 'hands-on' or 'hands-off' are they—can you use your own initiative?

— *Recognise and appreciate your boss's strengths.* Compliment your boss when they do something you like; that way they'll learn the actions and attitudes that work for you.

— *Remember, bosses are human too.* Bosses make mistakes too. If your boss is reasonable when you make a mistake then you should be prepared to do the same for them.

— *Perfect the art of compromise.* If you want to do something one way and your boss wants it done another, find out why, don't just argue to get your way. Choose which battles to fight and which to decline. If it's possible, and appropriate, negotiate.

6

Making Your Boss Laugh

It is by now common knowledge that health studies bear out the old adage that laughter is the best medicine. A good belly laugh will lower the blood pressure below normal resting rates for 45 minutes and laughing exercises the lungs, increases oxygen in the bloodstream and stimulates production of endorphins, the brain's built-in painkiller.

Laughter is good for the health of a business, too. The benefits of laughter at work are much the same as laughter anywhere else. Basically, laughing makes you feel good and it reduces stress. Doesn't it make sense to let more laughter into the workplace, the source of a lot of people's stress? In addition to stress relief, a little comic relief in the workplace can help build camaraderie. Creating and sharing inside jokes helps co-workers feel closer to one another, enhancing teamwork through a sense of common history.

Humour is a wonderful lubricant for business relationships. The key is to use humour to strengthen relationships instead of to weaken them. Except the usual jokes exchanged with colleagues, business people tend to take things pretty seriously, maybe too seriously. In fact, companies are increasingly recognising that business success can be a laughing matter. The list of companies that have tried to incorporate more humour into the workplace continues to grow; it includes such corporate giants as General Electric, AT&T, Kodak, Lockheed and IBM. Even the Internal Revenue Service has taken steps to inject laughter into the workplace. Corporations often turn to humour consultants to help them lighten up.

Having a sense of humour has more to do with being able to see that there are funny situations all around us and feeling secure enough to laugh at them than it does with entertaining others. One big rule of thumb for humour in the workplace is to know your audience and make sure that your jocularity won't be seen as offensive, either because it is "dirty" or because it makes certain groups of people the butt of the joke.

Some bosses act as though they're allergic to humour, bristling when employees joke around in the office and fretting over the line between humour and harassment. But studies have proved that joking around on the job can actually have a positive effect on productivity and employee retention. The use of humour, and the ability to produce and make humour, is associated with intelligence and creativity, two things highly valued in workplaces. More important, the link between humour and positive emotions seems strong, which is intuitive, and there's also a strong correlation between positive emotions and workplace performance.

No one has really studied humour as an important part of employee performance directly, but we do know that positive affect in the workplace increases individual performance. And humour is one of the things associated with a positive affect, which increases not only productivity, but also the ability to communicate well with the boss, co-workers, and customers. It also enhances the degree to which you feel bonded, cohesive, and part of the group in the workplace. That's where employee retention comes into it. If you have positive emotions about your job, you're less likely to quit. And maybe part of that is because of the fun you're having in the break room. You might get a better job offer, but it will take more to draw you away when you like where you work and you like the people you work with.

The primary theory about humour, which is well accepted, is that it stems from incongruity. In other words, we find jokes or comments funny because they are linking two things together—perhaps through a punch line—that you wouldn't normally link together, or that shouldn't go together. Essentially, that's what creativity is, too: Putting things together in a unique way, like using the Internet for something people wouldn't have thought of before.

Developing a great sense of humour is a commitment. If you wanted to be a good golfer, it's not likely you'd think that reading one article would do the job. So it is with humour. Here are a few thoughts on impressing the boss with humour which will get you started and point you in the right direction.

ANALYSE YOUR BOSS'S SENSE OF HUMOUR

If your boss likes cartoons, wouldn't it make sense to clip a great cartoon when you see one and attach it to a memo? Does the boss laugh? Does he tell jokes? Does he smile? Just because your boss doesn't tell jokes doesn't mean that he or she doesn't have a sense of humour. He may be a carrier of humour, rather than a creator or initiator of humour. He may be the first one to laugh at someone else's jokes. It's also a possibility that your boss may never laugh at jokes and yet appreciate and enjoy humour. Everyone's humour personality is different.

If your boss seems to like off-colour humour, you have to avoid using that style of humour yourself. If he tends to tell or laugh at sex jokes, it's still unlikely that he will want the person he promotes to sales manager to be a teller of sex jokes or bodily function humour. For an upward-bound career, keep your humour clean and know your audience. Blue humour is a comedy-cop out. It's too easy to tell a sex joke. Leave that style of humour to the lazy and less inspired. You can do better.

UNDERSTAND WHAT MAKES HUMOUR TICK

Humour is primarily about surprise and relationships. One of the basic principles of telling a joke is keeping the punchline and punchword disguised until the end of the joke. The punchword is the word that triggers the laugh. Ideally it should be the last word you say.

A critical concept of humour is relationships. A good joke or cartoon is almost always a connection of two previously unrelated thoughts. The humour connected two previously unrelated signs. Get into the habit of looking for connections and relationships. It's the number one skill for creating your own humour.

Most humour in the business setting is unplanned. It just happens. Spontaneous events with clients and co-workers create the surprises and uncomfortable situations which call for humour as a coping tool. Regardless of where you are now, you can increase your humour skills. When you study humour, it's obvious there's more to it than just spontaneous laughs. There are times when you may want to deliberately use humour, maybe even plan it in advance. Perhaps you want to spice up a training session or a planning meeting. Maybe you want to lighten up a sales presentation. You can learn ways to administer a dose of laughter to help you connect and communicate.

There are three elements which can help you understand and structure your humour: surprise, tension and relationships.

First, humour is based on the element of surprise. Humour often comes from something as simple as someone saying the unexpected. The surprise twist creates the humour. Because of the element of surprise, when we are deliberately structuring a piece of humour we don't want to telegraph the joke. A line like, "a funny thing happened to me on the way over here," signals your listeners that a joke is coming. This will lessen the element of surprise.

To enhance the surprise, it's best to place the punch line at the end of the joke. And within the punch line, the punch word is usually given last. The punch word is the word that makes the humour work. It's the trigger that releases the surprise. If your humour falls flat, do what professional humourists do. Pretend you are serious. Since the listeners didn't realise you were making a joke, you never need to apologise or explain it. Turn your surprise into a secret.

It's no surprise to people who work in pressure-packed work environments that humour is also based on this second principle: release of tension. Laughter is a pressure valve which releases muscle tension. Uncomfortable situations, fear and pain are all tension builders that cry out for humour. We find ourselves laughing at risqué humour and embarrassing situations because they make us uncomfortable. We release the tension they create with humour.

People who intentionally and frequently use humour know tension can be used deliberately to heighten the impact of the humour. A pause placed just before the punch line or the punch word builds a sense of anticipation, a form of tension, which makes the joke stronger. In most jobs, daily challenges give you the opportunity to purposely use tension in setting up your humour. Simply by sharing a real life humourous situation, you can recreate the spontaneous circumstances which generated the laughter in the first place. Although there's nothing like "being there," you can improve on the actual event by embellishing to create a little more tension in the set up. You can structure the punch line for maximum effect by putting the punch word last. And you can pause to add impact.

As we plan our humour, we also notice that the third principle of humour is relationships. Most humour is based on how things are related and not related. We can create humourous twists when we play with relationships.

Natural, spontaneous humour is one of your greatest tools for coping with stress as you work. By understanding what makes the humour tick, you can become better at planning and deliberately using this powerful adjunct to your success arsenal.

GIVE SHAPE TO YOUR HUMOUR

Your humour skills get stronger with exercise. Getting in better shape takes work. And improving your sense of humour takes work too. It's about commitment and focus. Even if you just set aside just a half hour to develop some funny lines...you'll be preparing your mind to be funnier in the future. Step into the humour gym and give yourself a workout.

TAKE MIND VACATIONS

To make your boss laugh you have to be in a state of fun, to be relaxed. It's hard to be funny when you're stressed out. When you're tense, you're humour tends to be negative. Sarcastic humour is the result of frustration and tension. It works against you.

Here are some ideas to keep your mind, and humour, on a higher plane:

(a) *Keep something that makes you laugh or smile near your phone.* When you get placed on hold for thirty seconds, flip open your favourite book of humour writings or cartoons to lighten the moment.

(b) *Have a fun photo on your desk, something that recalls wonderful memories.* Maybe you have a picture of your kids at Disney World. Maybe a picture of your last year's Halloween costume. Perhaps a photo will remind you that your dog makes you laugh.

(c) *Consider breaking the pattern when you're in a stressful mood.* Do something differently. If you've been with people, spend some time alone. If you've been sitting, take a walk. If you've been in a quiet environment, go someplace stimulating. If you've been indoors, step outside. Whenever you're stressed, your body is usually telling you that you need to do something differently.

(d) *Help design a better break room.* This will provide a place for you and your co-workers to have a mini-vacation. Find some fun posters to decorate the room. Furnish the room with fun games and puzzles. Design a bulletin board for fun photos, cartoons and contests. You'll make the work environment more fun for you and for everyone else. The boss will like that.

PHYSICAL AND EMOTIONAL ASPECTS

If you want to feel like you're having fun, act like you are. If your physical posture is depressed, it will be hard to be funny. One of the keys to developing a great smile is to do some mirror work. We just don't know what a good smile feels like. By doing mirror practice, your goal is to create muscle memory, to be able to recreate that great looking smile.

Story Power

A great way to impress your boss with humour is to be great-at telling personal stories. With this skill you can earn the reputation as a great leader, motivator or sales professional. Telling a story is the perfect way to build one-on-one relationships and a terrific way to bring a speech alive. Start by keeping a humour journal. Record every funny thing that happens to you. You'll discover that funny stuff happens to you more frequently. Actually that's not true. What really happens is that you become more tuned to the funny stuff that would have normally gone unnoticed. Then practice telling your stories your friends and family. When you tell stories, one of the most effective forms of humour is poking fun at yourself. Humour targeted at you is almost always safe material. Stories coming from your own experiences will be original and fun to listen to. People like others who don't take themselves too seriously.

Become a Funny Summariser

Set a goal for yourself. Every time you attend a staff meeting, try to create a piece of observational humour by the end of the meeting. This doesn't mean you always will use it. But when the timing seems right, weave your humour gem into your closing remarks. You'll get better over time. And eventually you'll gain a reputation for being a very funny person. People will learn to listen to you every time you speak. This is hot tip number two. Observational humour skills are powerful.

Show your sense of humour in other ways: By a toy on your desk, by a plaque on your wall, by a bumper sticker on your car, by the books on your shelf. There are ways to show your appreciation for and enjoyment of humour without being a jokester. Wear a funny shirt on casual day.

Don't Try too Hard

The harder you try to be funny, the less funny you'll be. When you try really hard to be funny you appear to come from a place of need. You appear to be desperately craving attention. And that's not funny. When you try some humour, just throw it out there as though you were simply testing it. If nobody laughs, pretend you were serious. If you do it right, nobody will know. After all, the best humour comes as a surprise. So since your boss wasn't looking for something funny, if you weren't funny, then he won't have a clue that you were expecting to be. Don't beg for laughs. Just let it go and learn from it.

SECRETS OF OFFICE HUMOUR

Here are some tips on making sure your attempts at humor don't cross the line and turn you into a Fool.

1. *Start slowly*. If you jump right in with a hefty dose of humor, you're likely to make others uncomfortable and alienate potential supporters, no matter how harmless it may seem.
2. *Think first*. Before you launch any kind of practical joke, consider whether it really will be funny for all involved. If it's likely to make others feel the need to "get even," you're better off calling it off before a vicious cycle begins.
3. *Play it safe*. If you're not sure whether a particular joke or shenanigan is appropriate, it probably isn't.

4. *Be respectful* .This doesn't mean you can't poke fun at people from time to time, but only by respecting them first and foremost can you have fun without offending or alienating.
5. *Check for negativity*. Poking fun at someone as a way to vent negative feelings isn't funny, and can injure inter-office relationships.
6. *Avoid sensitive topics*. Jokes about someone's weight, age, intelligence, or other personal characteristics have the potential to hurt self-esteem — and should be absolutely off-limits.
7. *Excel first*. When you're competent, people respect you, and you can have fun at what you do. But if you're not doing a good job, using humor may work against you and make otherwise innocent fun seem out of place or, worse yet, downright offensive.
8. *Don't get carried away*. Remember, even where humour is concerned, your best bet is to focus on taking yourself lightly and your work seriously.

Office humour is a wonderful thing that can bring workers and boss together and relieve tension and stress. With these guidelines you will have your boss and colleagues chuckling without offending anyone.

7

How to Say No to Your Boss

Saying yes is easy, saying no is a skill. And an important skill too, because saying yes too often can get you into trouble and saying nothing is troublesome altogether. So saying no is an important skill to use on a regular basis.

Saying no to a person holding the power of employment or influence can be very challenging, but it is possible to say no and avoid adverse results. We say "yes" to boss because we want to please them. But when eventually we can't continue, we let them down and we feel guilty. Both parties suffer. Recognise that a desire to please often prevents us from saying no.

If you have a written set of goals and strategies, this gives you a reason to stick to your course. When someone persists, repeat your position, perhaps in a slightly different way. Make sure you understand exactly what is being asked of you before you respond. Perhaps the task is more time consuming than you thought.

Excel at just a few things, rather than being just average at many. Don't try to do everything. You have a right to say no. Remember that others may take you for granted and even lose respect for you if you don't. Be polite, but firm in saying no. You only build false hopes with wishy-washy responses. For instance, the phrase "I'll try to be there" in response to a party invitation is giving yourself an excuse to avoid a commitment. It doesn't do anyone any favours.

When a superior asks you to do a new urgent task. Remind her that you are working on other projects that she has already identified as top priorities. Ask for help in deciding where the new task should fall on the list of priorities. Point out that you might be able to do everything, but not to the usual high standards that are expected.

Some experts recommend keeping your answer short. This way, you can say no without feeling the need for a lengthy justification. On the other hand, others say that giving a longer answer with reasons reinforces your credibility. Let the situation decide.

Saying no is often associated with negative feelings, like disappointment, anger and loss. That is why it is a lot easier to say yes all the time, because people like to avoid situations that evoke those emotions. But at the same time, we don't feel proud or satisfied with saying yes. So often we reside to other options, but they prove to be even more troublesome than just saying no:

— *Saying yes, doing yes.* This is authentic. If you say yes, do yes. People will know that you keep your word.

— *Saying yes, doing no.* This is deception. You try to keep the relationship good at first, but don't keep your word and end up damaging it in the end.

— *Saying nothing, doing yes.* This is vague, but mostly if you do not answer people assume that you will say yes.

— *Saying nothing, doing no.* This is vague and deceptive. People assume that you say yes, but you do the opposite. Plenty of room for an argument.

— *Saying no, doing yes.* This is confusing to say the least. People will not know what your word is worth, saying no clearly does not mean no.

— *Saying no, doing no.* This is authentic. If you say no, do no. You might disappoint someone, but you are clear and people will know that you keep your word.

Saying yes and saying no are the only two viable options in the long run. Saying yes is something that most people are very capable of, saying no on the other hand. To master the skill of saying no, you need to build upon your courage and consideration. Courage is the skill you need for you. It is needed to be able to choose for yourself and say no when you feel or know you have to say no. You might disappoint someone, but you have the courage to bite the bullet and just say it.

Consideration is the skill you need for the other. Taking the needs and wants of the other into consideration is an important skill to assess the impact of saying no. It might not change your decision, but it will prepare you and allow you to get the message across in a respectful way.

Saying no needs consideration and respect for the other, because if it's not important to you, it doesn't mean it's not important altogether. Hear the other out as they are explaining why they want you to do something (seek first to understand). Repeat in your own words what you think they said, to confirm that you understood them (this will gratify them already). Tell them you understand why that's important to them, and explain them why you are going to say no nevertheless. If people feel understood, you have created fertile ground to say no respectfully. And people will appreciate you for it too. If you take it one step further, you can build upon what you just achieved. Explore the problem at hand for a moment to find another solution. Finding a new solution that serves both purposes is saying no too, but more creative. You say no to the lose and openly explore how to change it into a win. This will build your image of leadership even further.

Sometimes, saying no is simply unavoidable. Here are some techniques to use:

— Tell the person you can agree to their request this time, but ask how the two of you might plan better for the next time.

— Tell them yes, but remind them they owe you one. For example, they might cover you for a shift next time you need time off.

— Tell them yes, but take control by saying you'll come back to them with a timetable.

— Put a tough condition on your agreement. "If it would only take an hour, I'd be able to help, but I can't give you more than that."

Be honest with yourself. Is your plate piled too high with deadlines and obligations that you're trying to squeeze in between meetings? Are you trying to cram too many activities into too little time? If so, stress relief can be as straightforward as just saying no — or no more.

There are countless worthy requests out there just waiting to decrease the amount of free time you have, and increase your level of stress. So, it's easy to create stressful situations in your life, if you don't turn down requests for your time and talents.

Who will make costumes for the school play or coach your children's Little League team if you don't? The answer may not be simple, but you should still consider these reasons for making sure it's not you.

— *Saying no can be good for you.* Saying no is not a selfish act. In fact, it may be the most beneficial thing that you can do for your family and your other commitments. When you say no, you'll be able to spend quality time on the things you've already said yes to.

— *Saying no can allow you to try new things.* Just because you've always helped plan the company softball tournament doesn't mean that you have to keep doing it forever. Saying no will free up time to pursue other hobbies or interests.

— *Yes isn't always the best answer.* If you're over-committed and under a lot of stress, you've got a much better chance of becoming sick, tired or just plain old crabby, which doesn't benefit you or anyone else.

— *It's important to recognise the power of other people.* Let those around you come through. Although others may not do things exactly the same way you would, you can learn a valuable lesson by allowing others to help, while gaining treasured free time.

Sometimes it's tough to determine which activities deserve your time and attention. Use these strategies to evaluate obligations and opportunities that come your way.

— *Find yourself.* Saying no helps you prioritise the things that are important to you. You'll gain time that you can commit to the things that you really want to do, such as leaving work at a reasonable hour to make time for a mind-clearing run at the end of the day. Examine your current obligations and overall priorities before making any new commitments. Ask yourself if the new commitment is important to you. If it's something that you feel strongly about, by all means do it.

— *Weigh the yes-to-stress ratio.* Is the new activity that you're considering a short- or long-term commitment? Taking an afternoon to bake a batch of cookies for the school bake sale will take far less of your precious time than heading up the school fund-raising committee for an entire year. If an activity is going to end up being another source of stress in your life — especially for the long-term — take a pass.

— *Let go of guilt.* If friends want to get together for an imprompt evening out on the town when you've already scheduled a quiet evening at home with your partner, it's okay to decline their offer. Do what you've set out to do and don't veer off that path because of feelings of guilt or obligation. It will only lead to additional stress in your life.

— *Keep your current commitments in check.* If you have relatives coming over for dinner, don't go overboard. Order pizza or ask everyone to bring a dish to share.

— *Sleep on it.* Are you tempted by a friend's invitation to volunteer at your old alma mater or join a weekly golf league? Take a day to think over the request and respond after you've been able to assess your current commitments as well as the new opportunity.

Saying no won't be easy if you're used to saying yes all the time. But learning to say no is an important part of simplifying your way to a better, less stressful life.

WHY AND HOW TO SAY NO TO YOUR BOSS

Your boss just assigned a new project to you and you can't imagine how you'll get it done. Can you say no to your boss, though? You can if your reasons are good. Now, you have to decide if they are. First here are some questions you can ask yourself to help you decide. Following that are bad reasons to say no, and then good reasons. Then once you've made up your mind, there's advice on how to present your decision to your boss.

Questions to Ask Yourself Before Saying No to Your Boss

— Am I already working on several important assignments that leave me no time for this one?

— Can I delegate some of my other work to make room for this assignment?

— Can I put some of my other assignments on the back burner while I work on this one?

— Will taking on this assignment cause harm to my other work?

— Do I absolutely lack the skills necessary to complete this assignment?

— Am I the only person who can successfully complete this assignment?

Bad Reasons To Say No to Your Boss

Turning down an assignment from your boss is not something you should do on a whim. While the reasons listed here may seem important to you, they probably aren't good enough for your boss.

— The project looks too difficult.

— It isn't part of my job description.

— I'm in the middle of planning my wedding and can't focus on anything right now.

Good Reasons to Say No to Your Boss

Though you should give an assignment careful consideration before you turn it down, if your boss is fairly reasonable, he or she should be able to understand these reasons.

— There simply aren't enough hours in a day to work on it, even if I get to work early and stay late.

— My other work will suffer if I take on this assignment.

— I don't have the necessary skills to complete this project and I will not be able to attain them in time.

How to Say No to Your Boss

If you decide to turn down an assignment, be prepared to offer a good reason for doing so. You will have to explain your reasons thoroughly so your boss realises you considered the situation carefully. Give your boss ample warning so he or she has enough time to assign the work to someone else or can help you delegate some of your other projects to one of your co-workers so you can work on this one.

— If your reason for saying no to your boss is that you don't have enough time to work on the project, prepare a list of the other projects on which you're working. If he didn't delegate the other assignments to you, he may not even be aware of them. If he did assign the other projects, he may want you to work on the new one instead.

— If you think your other work will suffer if you take on another assignment, explain that to your boss. She will appreciate your honesty and your dedication to your other projects.

— If you don't have the necessary skills to complete this assignment, admit this to your boss. It would be worse to pretend you can do something you can't. Ask him if future assignments will require this skill. If his answer is "yes," let him know you will work to attain it.

Here are some things to keep in mind when you need to say no:

— *Practice full disclosure.* Don't fabricate reasons to get out of an obligation. The truth is always the best way to turn down a friend, family member or co-worker.

— *Let them down gently.* Many good causes land at your door, and it can be tough to turn them down. Complimenting the person or group's effort while saying that you're unable to commit at this time helps to soften the blow and keep you in good graces.

Saying no won't be easy if you're used to saying yes all the time. But learning to say no is an important part of simplifying your way to a better, less stressful life.

HOW TO SAY NO RESPECTFULLY

Turning down a friendly request can take nerve, but it's often necessary. When you can't or don't want to help out, get yourself together and kindly but firmly turn them down. Here are some tips for how to say no respectfully:

— Listen to the request respectfully. Do not interrupt the speaker.

— Phrase your "no" as simply as possible. Don't raise your voice or become upset, simply say that you cannot help this time. When you say no, say it in a confident, well modulated voice to sound more straight-foward.

— Don't feel obligated to explain. You have your reasons and they may not be ones you wish to discuss. If this is the case, try saying something like, "I realise you'd like me to explain more fully why I won't be able to do this, but just know that although I'd always like to be helpful to you, this time, I'm just not able to." Leave it at that—if you must, change the subject, or say, "I'm so sorry, but I need to go."

— Explain simply, and only if you wish to do so. If the case really is one that you feel okay explaining, make your explanation as simple as possible.

— Stand firm. If the requestor does not want to accept your answer, tell him or her that your mind is made up and that you will not change it.

— If you aren't the kind of person who says no face-to-face or at least talking live on the phone, than send an SMS or similar. This might help.

— Don't be submissive or dismissive. Be respectful. Even if they don't.

— Be aware of what sort of pressure might compromise your refusal. Plan ahead.

— If your refusal gives rise to anger, remain calm and, if possible, remove yourself from the situation.

— Do not lie when you explain why your answer is no.

— Preface your 'No' by saying 'I have heard you and understand your situation' before refusing—it helps if people feel empathy.

8

Dealing with Unhappy Moments

Dealing with unhappy moments with a boss is a big challenge many employees face. Almost everyone does have a bad boss at one time or another. When you have a bad boss, a bad boss is a significant factor in most people's lives. There are two kinds of bad bosses. One doesn't know they're bad. The other is bad to the bone.

The definition of "bad" depends on the employee's needs, the manager's skills and the circumstances. A hands-off manager may not realise that his failure to provide any direction or feedback makes him a bad boss. He may think he's empowering his staff. A manager who provides too much direction and micro-manages may feel insecure and uncertain about his own job. He may not realise his direction is insulting to a competent, secure, self-directed staff member. Or, maybe the boss lacks training and is so overwhelmed with his job requirements that he can't provide support for you. Perhaps he has been promoted too quickly or his reporting responsibilities have expanded beyond his reach. In these days of downsizing, responsibilities are often shared by fewer staff members than ever before.

This bad boss may not share your values. The newer generation of workers expect that they can use their vacation time and take action to make work-life balance a priority. Not all bosses share these views. If your values are out of sync with those of your boss, you do have a problem.

Recommended approach to the unwitting bad boss:

— Talk to this boss. Tell him what you need from him in term of direction, feedback and support. Be polite and focus on your needs. Telling the boss he's a bad boss is counterproductive and won't help you meet your goals.

— Ask the manager how you can help him reach his goals. Make sure you listen well and provide the needed assistance.

— Seek a mentor from among other managers or more skilled peers, with the full knowledge of your current manager, to enlarge your opportunity for experience.

— If you've taken these actions, and they haven't worked, go to your boss's manager and ask for assistance. Or, you can go to your Human Resources staff first, to rehearse and gain advice. Understand that your current boss may never forgive you, so ensure you have done what you can do with him, before taking your issues up the line.

— You may never hear what the boss's boss or the HR staff did to help solve your bad manager's behaviour. It's confidential. But, do allow some time to pass for the actions to have their desired impact.

— If nothing changes, despite your best efforts, and you think the problem is that they don't believe you, draw together coworkers who also experience the behaviour. Visit the boss's manager to help him see the size and impact of the behaviour.

— If you think the problem is that your boss can't—or won't—change, ask for a transfer to another department. This recommendation presumes you like your employer and your work.

— If a transfer or promotion is unavailable, begin your search for a new job. Fleeing is always an option. You may want to conduct your job search secretly, but under the circumstances, it may be time for you to go.

Working with a manager at a client company, we discussed his approach to employees. He looked down his nose at them. He criticised and screamed at employees. He publicly humiliated any employee who made a mistake. This manager thought his behaviour was perfectly acceptable. Most managers that bully, intimidate, cruelly criticise, name call and treat you as if you are stupid likely know what they are doing. They may know they're bad and even revel in their badness. They may feel their behaviour has been condoned—and even encouraged—within your organisation. They may have learned the behaviours from their former supervisor who was viewed as successful.

You don't have to put up with demeaning behaviour. You deserve a good boss who helps your self-confidence and self-esteem grow. You deserve a good boss who helps you advance your career. You deserve civil, professional treatment at work.

Recommended approach to deal with the bad boss who knows:

— Start by recognising that you have the right to a professional environment in your workplace. You are not the problem. You have a bad boss. He is the problem.

— You can try talking with the bad boss to tell him the impact that his actions or words are having on you or your performance. In a rare blue moon, the bad boss might care enough to work to modify his behaviour. If he does decide to work on his behaviour, hold him to his commitments. If you allow him to yell at you, even just a little bit, you are training him that he can get away with his former behaviour. Don't go to war publicly, but draw his behaviour to his attention as soon as you have the opportunity, privately.

— If the behaviour does not change, appeal to his supervisor and to Human Resources staff. Describe exactly what he does and the impact the behaviour is having on you and your job performance. You may never hear what the boss's boss or the human resource staff did to help solve your bad manager's behaviour. It's confidential. But, do allow some time to pass for the actions to have their desired impact.

— If nothing changes, despite your best efforts, and you think the problem is that they don't believe you, draw together coworkers who also experience the behaviour. Visit the boss's manager to help him see the size and impact of the behaviour.

— If you think the problem is that your boss can't or won't change, ask for a transfer to another department.

— If a transfer or promotion is unavailable, begin your search for a new job. Fleeing is always an option. You may want to conduct your job search secretly, but under the circumstances, it may be time for you to go.

WHAT MAKES A BAD BOSS

Bad bosses, in order of their frequency in the comments thread, do the following:

— Love brownnosers, tattletales, and relatives who report to them. They choose favourite employees and cover up and make excuses for the poor work of their incompetent favourites. They ignore selected people and discriminate against many employees.

— Fail to communicate, and may not even have, expectations, timelines or goals. Bad bosses change their minds frequently leaving employees off-balance. Bad bosses change expectations and deadlines frequently.

— Use disciplinary measures inappropriately when simple, positive communication would correct the problem. Bad bosses ignore employees until there is a problem, then pounce.

— Speak loudly, rudely, one-sidedly to staff. Bad bosses don't provide the air time for staff to respond to accusations and comments. They intimidate people and bully staff. They allow other employees to bully employees.

— Take credit for the successes and positive accomplishments of employees. They are equally as quick to blame employees when something goes wrong.

— Fail to provide rewards or recognition for positive employee performance.

These six were the top "bad boss" characteristics cited by readers. The following came up less frequently but were contributed by more than one reader. The bad boss:

— Is not qualified for the boss job by either skills or experience.

— Will not let go of problems or mistakes. The bad boss returns to discuss negative events continually and searches for faults in employees.

— Will not accept constructive feedback and suggestions for improvement. The bad boss can't deal with disagreement from employees who have their own opinions about work related issues.

— Lacks integrity, breaks promises, and is dishonest.

— Does not have the courage to deal with a difficult situation despite knowing that it is the right thing to do.

— Causes dissention among staff members by his or her actions and comments.

Reader comments also made the point that a lot of bad boss behaviour is enabled, or at least allowed, by the boss's bad boss.

DO'S AND DON'TS OF DEALING WITH A BAD BOSS

Follow these general rules for coping with a bad or ineffective boss.

— Do act professionally in all situations.

— Don't reduce your productivity, feign illness, or otherwise compromise your job.

— Do find a mentor—within or outside the organisation. Read more.

— Don't confront your boss in an emotionally-charged rant.

— Do consider scheduling a meeting with your boss to discuss ways your boss could change his/her behaviour.

— Don't go to the boss of your boss, except as a last resort.

— Do find an outlet to vent your frustrations and anger, but don't do it with co-workers.

— Don't expect your boss to change—or at least change overnight.

— Do watch for opportunities to transfer to another department within the company.

— Don't simply try and block out all the bad behaviour; doing so will impact your physical and mental health.

— Do use your network to keep abreast of better opportunities outside the company. And do have your resume up-to-date and ready to send out.

— Do evaluate your performance on the job and consider ways to improve your behaviour, but don't blame yourself for a bad boss.

— Don't think you are alone in having a bad boss; several studies suggest that many of us have to deal with a bad boss at one time or another in our careers.

— Do consider keeping a journal that documents all the bad behaviour of your boss.

— Don't sacrifice your health of self-esteem by staying in the job for the sake of a job. Do consider quitting your job—even if you don't have a new job lined up—if continuing to work for your bad boss is likely to permanently damage your career.

— Do continue to document all your accomplishments.

HOW TO DEAL WITH AN ABSENTEE BOSS

Most of us wish our bosses weren't breathing down our necks every day. Yet if you talk to anyone whose boss is constantly on the road, you'll hear complaints of last-minute phone calls from off-site, changing travel locations and dates, and deadline changes from the field to meet clients' demands. Many on-the-road bosses complain they can never get their assistants on the phone when they most need to. A cell phone is a saviour, but many people turn them off during meetings or in areas with bad reception. Meanwhile, you should be on another call or away from your desk. There are several ways to set up an effective communication system with a gypsy boss:

— Make phone calls from your boss a top priority by alerting the receptionist and anyone else who answers phones to page you if you don't answer your line when the boss calls.

— If you do miss a call from your boss, agree to have a 10 to 20-minute system for you to call back. That means he'll leave the number where you can reach him within the next 10 to 20 minutes. Or have the boss leave you a time and phone number to call later.

— If the above systems fail, get a cell phone exclusively for communication with your boss. Always keep it with you during business hours and don't give the number to family or friends. This is a constant hot-line for your boss's calls.

Having your boss out of town creates the impression that you have time to help out other managers. Don't get trapped by your good will — many assistants don't set firm boundaries between themselves and other managers so they wind up with other people's work. Here are some rules for when your boss is out of town:

— Follow a strict schedule. This includes your casual coffee break schedule as well as time spent on your serious things-to-do list.

— Be prepared to draw a line in the sand professionally. Your boss isn't there to help protect you from aggressive coworkers who may try to take advantage of your "ghost boss" situation. If someone asks you to work on something, weigh the favour and defend your time. Will meeting the request interfere with deadlines you must meet for your boss? Will it put you at risk of missing your boss's call? If it's just a minor favour to pitch in on something, think about helping out. If it's a bigger request and you can't do it, explain why you don't have time.

— Take orders for big projects only from your boss. If you let your boss allow others to start giving you work, confusion will reign, deadlines will conflict and you'll never know who's in charge.

— Monitor your own behaviour. Without someone watching you every day, it's easy to stop using your time wisely. Monitoring your behaviour so that you always act professionally is crucial if you're to be perceived as a hard worker. Do you take advantage of your boss's absence by having long lunches? Would you chat so much with coworkers if he were there? Keep a log of how your time is spent, and make sure you're putting in a full day.

The bottom line is if your boss is out of the office, it's up to you to manage things. Take charge of your job, and make sure the communication lines between you and your boss are always open.

DEALING WITH AN ABUSIVE BOSS

What should you know if you're the victim of an abusive boss? Here are today's five tips.

1. Identify the Behaviour

There are all kinds of abusive bosses. The Institute classifies them a few different ways. There are the constant critics who use put-downs, insults and name-calling. They may use aggressive eye contact to intimidate. There are also two-headed snakes who pretend to be nice, while all the while trying to sabotage you. Then there are the gatekeepers — people who are obsessed with control — who allocate time, money and staffing to assure their target's failure. Control freaks ultimately want to control your ability to network in the company or to let your star shine.

2. Don't Take it Lying Down

If your boss has a difficult management style, you don't have to let their bad behaviour go. You can respond — just remember to stay professional. If you find out that your boss is bad-mouthing you to higher-ups in the company, confront them directly and professionally. Get the evidence in writing from your source if you can. Then, ask him or her what is causing them to do this. You could say, "I've been hearing from other people in the company that you're not happy with my work, you and I know that this isn't the case and I want to talk about how we can fix this."

If your boss has been defaming you, that's illegal. You may want to consult an attorney. If your boss is a control freak who's breathing down your neck, you should address it. If someone screams at you, don't be a doormat. If you've made a mistake, acknowledge it. But let your boss know that they're creating a difficult work environment. Even if you haven't made a mistake, you may want to calmly ask what they're upset about and if you can address it.

3. Take Notes

Documenting your boss's bad behaviour is key for two reasons.

First, you might not even realise the extent of the problem. Taken in isolation, these events may seem trivial, but taken as a whole, it often becomes more clear what's actually going on. Some victims may be in denial or discount these events as isolated incidents. Your written records can document how severe the situation is. And, of course, if you decide to take legal action down the line, you may need the information. It's best to document these incidents as soon as possible so they're fresh in your mind.

Documentation is also important if you plan to report the behaviour to your boss's boss or to your company's human resources department. And don't dismiss the idea of taking the bull by the horns and working toward a solution. Try arranging a face-to-face meeting with your boss. Tell them you want to discuss the problems you've encountered because you want to resolve them. Chances are often slim that this will work, however. If they reject the opportunity to discuss things with you, add that to your documentation.

4. Know When It's Too Much

Bosses may exhibit bad behaviour sometimes. Hey, no one is perfect, not even bosses. But if your boss is abusing you, that's a problem. The problem takes on greater urgency if the abuse starts to make you feel bad. If you chronically suffer high blood pressure that started only when you began working for your boss; or you feel nauseous the night before the start of the work week; or if all your paid vacation days have been used up for mental health breaks.

When the bullying has had a prolonged affect on your health or your life outside of work, it's time to get out. It's also time to leave if your confidence or your usual exemplary performance has been undermined. Ironically, targets of abusive bosses tend to be high achievers, perfectionists and workaholics. Often bully bosses try to mask their own insecurities by striking out.

5. Control Your Destiny

Even after you leave your nightmare boss, you'll still have to explain why you left to potential new employers. One way to gracefully sidestep the issue: say you and your manager had a long-standing disagreement over the most effective way of getting things done and you thought the most professional way to resolve it was to move on.

"You certainly don't want to start recalling and recounting the abuse you suffered. You'll inevitably get upset and that's not the way you want to handle a job interview," she says.

Try to control the interview situation to the extent you can. Don't give your abusive boss as a reference but rather someone else with whom you worked previously. Another good choice might be a colleague or a peer you're on good terms with or someone who can speak about you professionally. Also, if you only worked for your bullying boss for a short time, you may want to consider leaving that job off your resume altogether.

WHEN YOUR BOSS IS A BULLY

The steady flow of uncertain news about the economy indicates that companies are under tremendous pressure to improve profits. No question, that pressure is felt all the way up and down the management line.

Hard times sometimes bring out the best in people, but anxious times can also bring out the bullies lurking in corporate ranks. There are several flavours of bad bosses, but bullies are the ones who misuse their power over others. They verbally abuse you, humiliate you in front of others.

Bully bosses over-control, micro-manage, and display contempt for others, usually by repeated verbal abuse and sheer exploitation. They look over your shoulder. They constantly put others down, with snide remarks or harsh, repetitive, and unfair criticism. They don't just differ with you, they differ with you contemptuously; they question your adequacy and your commitment. They spew on people in support functions, on competitors, perhaps even their own bosses.

Nowadays, most bullies are weeded out before they get to the very top of big companies, but they thrive in the mid ranks, and at all ranks of smaller firms, where the quality of management suffers due to the absence of professional managers.

Bad bosses are often very bright workers. And therein lies the problem. They make a significant contribution to the company as workers. They get promoted because of their technical proficiency and expertise. And they wind up supervising others. As long as you do things their way, you're a winner. But they don't generate innovation — and if there's one thing companies need today it's constant innovation. Bullies do a lot of damage in companies. They keep you in a state of psychological emergency. Add to it the rage you feel towards the bully and a sense of self-rage for putting up with such behaviour — hardly prime conditions for doing your best work, or any work at all.

It's never easy to make headway with an office bully. But here are some tactics culled from experts that could help you handle bully bosses.

- Confront the bully. "I'm sorry you feel you have to do that but I will not put up with that kind of behaviour. It has no place here." It can be startlingly effective. A bully can't bully if you don't let yourself be bullied.
- Conduct the confrontation in private — behind closed doors. A bully won't back down in front of an audience.

— Specify the behaviour that's unworkable. "You cannot just fire from the hip and demean me in front of other workers."

— Don't play armchair psychologist. Focus the discussion on specific behaviours, not theories of why you think the boss does it.

— Make your boss aware of the consequences of his or her behaviour on others. "I've been noticing how Peter seems so demoralised lately. I think a contributing factor may be last week's meeting when you ridiculed him for producing an inadequate report."

— Awareness is good but not enough; help your boss figure out what to do. Specify the behavioural change you want and supply an example of desirable behaviour—from the boss' own repertoire of actions. Jump in with "I can recall a month ago when you were ... lavish in your praise of that new assistant," or whatever.

— Point out how the boss's behaviour is seen by others. "You embarrass me when you publicly humiliate me in a meeting, but you also embarrass yourself. You're demonstrating your weakness."

— Try humour. If you point out to your boss that she's acting like a cartoon caricature, that may be enough to make her aware.

— Recruit an ally or allies. Standing up for yourself can stop a bully by earning his/her respect. But it could also cost your job. The higher your boss is in the organisation, the more you need allies. Check out with other workers whether the behaviour you are experiencing is generalised. If it is, it's easier for two or three people to confront a boss than one alone.

— If you are important to the organisation, you may accomplish your goal by going to your boss's boss.

DEALING WITH A GABBING BOSS

Most complaints about bosses' communication styles are about those who communicate too little. There are a few, though, who just want to gab. They don't have anything to say, they just gab. It's a serious problem for your boss, but you don't have to let it become a problem for you.

Since your boss is out of bounds, direct requests that the gabbing stop will likely be experienced as criticism or attack. A defensive response or even retribution are probable outcomes. Hinting is dangerous for the same reason, but since hints are less clear, the message is also less likely to arrive. Your boss hasn't asked for your help.

Refrain from providing "feedback" or "advice" unless you're asked. Not only is it risky when your boss is involved, but it rarely works unless the person in question asks for it. The problem might be only temporary If, in your workplace, actual job performance and performance evaluation are correlated, your boss is probably in trouble. Habitually spending so much time so unproductively can't help. If you can wait long enough, the problem will go away, because you'll have a new boss.

Is there a time of day when you're more likely to be targeted? If so, be sure to be somewhere else if you can. If you can't see a pattern, keep a log—you'll know for sure after a few weeks. Exploit meeting scheduling software. Look up your boss's schedule, and plan to be somewhere else when he or she is free. Schedule meetings for those times, or work in a conference room if you can.

Consider time-shifting your hours. If your boss is a morning person, arrive later. If you can telecommute on some days, do. If asked why you suddenly changed your schedule, say something about "so many interruptions." Keep it impersonal. Sign a mutual assistance treaty. If others are also affected by your boss's chat habit, make a pact with someone else: if you see your boss chatting with your pal, put in a phone call to break up the conversation. Have your pal do the same for you.

If all else fails, pick up your coffee cup and say, "I need some more coffee." Stand, take a step, turn back, and say, "Join me?" Most people will leave your office with you — few will accompany you to the coffee station. If he or she does tag along, continue the conversation, lingering in a public place — don't return to your office. That will usually force a quick end, and you can get back to work.

TYPES OF BOSSES YOU NEED TO AVOID

Here are some basic advice on the types of bosses you should avoid:

Boss without a Personal Life

This boss suffers from "everyone should suffer like me" syndrome. There are bosses out there that have little in their lives besides work and don't respect the fact that others do. To avoid facing the empty and joyless lives they have, they typically glorify work as if it's the only thing worth doing.

These bosses will not hesitate to ask you to work on Poker Night or cancel your family vacation to hill-station. You can tell you have one of these bosses if you see them running to the crapper, bringing along a memo to read, so they don't miss a second of work time. If you have one of these work all the time types, go find a new boss or watch your life dry up like dog poop in the sun.

Boss Who Wants to Piss You

This boss suffers from "if I am nasty, no one will notice I am stupid" syndrome. There are bosses out there who don't know how to say "thank you" or "great job". Silent when you perform and deliver well, they are the first to publicly berate you with a warm stream of criticism for mistake. Fearful of being discovered for the failures that they are, they will leap at the chance to make others look bad.

Boss Who Constantly Clowns Around

This boss suffers from "I am a laughing fool" syndrome. When you first meet this type of boss, you'll think they're great. You love the idea of having a fun boss to work with at first. Only when you've been with them a while do you realise that they are having too much fun to do any work. They are the ones spending all their work hours looking for a new gag to play or titillating gossip to spread around. Since they have little time to actually do their jobs, you will end up staying late every night to finish up their work. If you have a joker for a boss, you need to run far away from that circus.

Boss Who Struggles to Stay Afloat

Some managers are merely around to prove that the Peter Principle (that you get promoted until you get a job you can't do well and get stuck there) is alive and well in corporate America. Clueless as to how to do their job and afraid to admit it, they are always looking for someone to save them. Watch out as these bosses will surely cover up their incompetence by taking credit for your work and quickly toss you over to explain away their missed deadlines and bad decisions. If you have one these bosses, don't keep throwing them a life raft. Just let them flail around until they run out of energy and let them drown.

Boss Who Constantly Blows His Own Horn

This boss suffers from "if I say I am great enough times, it'll be true" syndrome. These bosses believe that if no one is saying anything nice about them, they should fill the void by creating loud fanfare about themselves. They are usually the ones who will tell you that the company can't survive without them. Needing constant polishing and buffing, they surround themselves with people who will support their delusions of grandeur. You can tell you have one of these bosses, if it feels like you are expected to start a parade every time they successfully go to the bathroom. If you have one of these bosses, tell them that you will no longer be part of the show and a member of their failing band.

Boss Competing With You

This boss suffers from "I need to prove I am not the weakest link" syndrome. Have you ever had a boss that makes everything a competition? These are the jerks that can't just be happy with the fact that they rule over your workday. They need to get the daily ego boost of winning, even it's just proving they can eat a sandwich faster than you.

Boss Having Verbal Diarrhoea

This boss suffers from "diarrhoea of the mouth" syndrome, constantly spewing dribble until nothing is left. These are the bosses that walk around telling everyone their pathetically unfunny story or joke of the day. They are the ones that need to take over every meeting, forcing everyone to swallow their bull. For these bosses, sucking up time is what they do best. These big mouths also tend to be backstabbing hypocrites, telling you how great you are to your face as they snicker over your latest goof with everyone else in the office. If you have one these bosses, tell them to shut their big gaping trap and tell their story to someone else.

Boss Who is Always on Tour

This boss suffers from "if I pretend to be busy, you'll find someone else" syndrome. There are bosses that are zipping around, never in one place long enough to actually do any work. These bosses often travel a lot and complain about it but find every opportunity to get out of the office. With the frenzy that surrounds them and their packed appointment book, there is no time to spare for a lowly slug like you. They are very good at delegating tasks and you are unsure as to whether they can do anything else but shove more work on you as they leave the office for one more trip. If you have one these bosses, use them for inspiration and zip yourself go somewhere else.

Boss Who is Sexy

This boss suffers from "I never get any at home so all I can do is talk about it" syndrome. Every workplace seems to have the office letch. The pig that has to leer and make a sexual comments every time someone attractive walks by. They are the first to note that a "sweater" is nice, as they stare at your breasts or tell you they are waiting for a big "package" to be delivered, as they lick their lips and look at your crotch. It's bad enough to have to deal with them at work but it's unbearable when they are your boss. Trying to look up your skirt when you're crossing your legs if you're hot (or making you feel like a cow chip if you are not), they can be relied upon to offer blush-worthy commentary on everything. You can tell you have one of these bosses if everything they say is filled with sexual innuendo and they even talk about the toilet as some sexual conquest.

If you have let's talk dirty boss, you should get another. It will only be a matter of time before you participate in the lewd talk to fit in, only to find charges of sexual harassment brought against you. Your boss will be too important to fire but you won't be.

Boss Who Will Eat You Alive

There are those bosses that are simply terrors to work with. Impatient, nasty and mean, they dismiss all of your contributions and belittle you at every turn. These bosses are great yellers, and when you think of them, all you can think of is a big snarling mouth. This type of boss won't hesitate to throw a tantrum, scream profanities as they smash things around the office and hurl books and pencils at you. If you have a man-eating boss, you need to break free from their nasty grasp. Life is too short to work for someone that's not even worthy of licking your toilet bowl so flush them away like the turds they are.

DEALING WITH A BOSS WITH POOR SUPERVISORY SKILLS

You know that promotion to supervisor is often a reward for a good worker. Remember that the "Peter Principle" suggests that people are often promoted to their level of incompetence. The Principle is still alive and well in corporate America. Here are a few clues that your boss could use some basic supervisory skills training.

— He ignores the classic, time honoured cliche, "Praise in public, criticise in private."

— She gives you assignments and doesn't follow up.

— He doesn't support you when something goes wrong.

— She thinks everything is fine when it isn't.

— He constantly claims that he is empowering you, but isn't.

— She micro-manages and needs to know everything.

— He acts paranoid.

— She jumps to conclusions.

— He doesn't know how to plan, prioritise or organise.

— If it isn't her idea, then it can't be good.

— He implements two-faced attacks.

— She tells sarcastic jokes or teases.

Now that you've come to the conclusion that your boss doesn't lie awake at night thinking about how to torment you, is there anything you can do? One activity that may be a cathartic experience is to make a list of the supervisory skills you think he or she is missing. Next, rank the list from most annoying to least annoying. Pick the top two or three worst offences. Recognise that these are your hot buttons and start developing a strategy. Don't wait for these things to happen again without having a plan for your own actions. The worst thing you can do is—nothing, hoping the problems will resolve themselves.

Don't sacrifice your health or self-esteem. Polite confrontation should always be your first move. However, a bad boss lacking supervisory skills may not recognise your attempt and this tactic may backfire. Limiting contact may help you personally but isn't usually a good professional move. However, putting some distance between you and your supervisor might be a temporary solution.

Here are a few other suggestions for dealing with a bad boss with poor supervisory skills:

— Find someone you can trust for a sanity check. It is probably better if this person does not work in the same environment as you.

— Make a pact with yourself that you will use the time to adopt good supervisory skills yourself.

— Remember that the best employees don't always make the best supervisors.

— Do not fret if you have experienced a total meltdown with this person; it is time to try a new strategy: forgiveness. Regain your strength and move forward with confidence and professionalism.

— Start identifying other sources of positive reinforcement for doing your job to the best of your abilities. We all want approval and recognition for a job well done.

HOW TO COPE WHEN YOUR ENEMY BECOMES YOUR BOSS

In a perfect world, everyone in corporate world would get along. There would be no interoffice bickering, no gossip, and no brutal competition among coworkers. In the real world, however, all of these things exist. If you are like most people, you have had at least one real work enemy in your career. This might be the person who always steals your thunder when you deserve the recognition, someone who is shameless in his or her pursuit of the corner office, or someone who just rubs you the wrong way. It may be easy to deal with or ignore an enemy in the workplace if he or she is your peer, but what if this person suddenly becomes your supervisor? Here are five ways to handle this challenging situation.

1. *Examine your own attitude and feelings toward your new boss.* If you consider this person an enemy for reasons such as jealousy or the two of you just haven't clicked, you need to make some adjustments to your own attitude. Do some real soul searching. Why don't you like this person? Are there ways you can get past your own negative

feelings? The company executives have obviously seen things in this person that they like, and it might be time for you to see his or her good qualities as well. Try to think of the good of the company, rather than yourself personally—you might even learn some things from your new boss.

2. *Be the bigger person.* Setting aside differences is sometimes extremely difficult, especially when it comes to work situations. But you may have to in order to succeed with your new leader. Think of it this way—your success at work depends, for the most part, on you. Focus your energy back on your tasks and development. Make a list of ways you can advance in your own career. Develop goals for finding more success within yourself and rise above the differences and any negative comments or interactions with your new supervisor.

3. *Dot your i's and cross your t's.* If your new boss has done things in the past to harm your career, you should definitely take more proactive steps to protect yourself. For example, if this person got his or her promotion from stepping on you and others in your office, document your work and copy others on projects, reports and other original work you have done. Keep a file with dated copies and include headers and footers that clearly show your were the original author. If your boss engages in unethical behaviour, you may need to collect solid evidence and share this with your human resources department. Even if he or she has not done anything so obvious, it is still a good idea to have a conversation with your HR department, if only to get your concerns on record. Be sure to approach this meeting respectfully and professionally. You do not want to come off as just a bitter employee who is jealous of another's success.

4. *Be open and honest.* If you think you and your new boss's differences can be resolved, request a meeting with him or her before you start your new working relationship. Sit down and talk about your differences and come up with ways to put them behind you. Remember that there are always two sides to every story, so be open to the other person's thoughts and perspective. You might find that your work enemy felt slighted by you. If you approach your relationship with an open mind and with the willingness to call a truce, you and your new boss will both feel more comfortable.
5. *If nothing else works, look to other options.* If you cannot let go of your differences, or if your boss is truly out to get you, your best option might be to make a more drastic change. Apply or post for a position in a different department or group. If you go this route, make sure you do so professionally and don't bad-mouth your supervisor. If you take your request to the HR department, you'll want to voice your concerns in a way that is taken seriously by the company. Avoid name-calling and unfounded accusations. If your company is unresponsive, you may need to look elsewhere for a new position.

CURING TOUGH BOSS SYNDROME

Do you have a boss who:

— Changes priorities often (usually without informing or consulting with you)?

— Doesn't give you regular feedback on your work, so you have no way of knowing whether or not you're meeting expectations?

— Never shows appreciation for a job well done?

— Micro-manages every little thing to the nth degree?

— Is a "big picture" type, giving you a vague idea about what needs to be done, but no real direction?

If any of the above scenarios sound familiar, you're probably suffering from Tough Boss Syndrome. Don't despair; the power of the cure lies within you. You can empower yourself to improve the situation.

The key is influence, which is not manipulation, but rather the ability to shape another person's behaviour in a positive way. Most tough boss problems centre on communication. You can get the results you want and build a better relationship with your boss when you influence him or her to communicate with you more effectively.

Ask yourself the following nine questions:

1. *How does my boss like to receive information?* What's the best way to deliver information to your boss-e-mail, hard copy memo or face to face? The easiest way to find out is simply to ask. Also seek the advice of peers who have already established successful relationships with the same boss.
2. *How much should I involve my boss?* Some bosses want to know everything and to be consulted on every decision. These micro-managers have a strong need for control. Other bosses prefer a more hand-off approach. While you can't change someone's personality, you can find ways to influence them to tell you exactly what they need to know in order to feel comfortable in the workplace.
3. *How can I solve my boss's problems?* Like it or not, your boss's problems are your problems. If you can figure out what keeps your boss awake at night and then find ways to help solve those problems, you will become more valuable and, so, more

influential. You can't force your boss to disclose problems but you can say, "If there's something you want to talk to me about, I'm available to listen. I have the skills to help you in areas relating to (X). If you think so, too, let's discuss how I can be of assistance."

4. *How can I make my needs clear to my boss?* Don't be shy about asking for what you want. If it lies within your boss's power to give it to you, that is, more responsibility, coaching or a corner office, ask for it. You may initially have to work up your nerve to ask, but your action will earn the respect of your boss, even a tough one. A majority of bosses say that they wish that their employees would just come right out and ask for what they want instead of being evasive, timid or passive-aggressive about their needs.

5. *Do I want more responsibility or less?* Would additional responsibility give you a sense of accomplishment and make your job more interesting? Or are you so overburdened and stressed out that you'd like to limit your responsibilities? Either way, you need to ask for what you want.

   Responsibility also means not being a victim. Responsible people make changes when they find themselves in a bad situation. When you don't take responsibility for making a change or getting what you need, you end up blaming your boss, the organisation or your co-workers. Always ask yourself, "What can I do to improve this situation?"

6. *How can I make my boss's job easier?* Influence and negotiation are very similar. You can make your boss's job easier by taking on some tasks that he or she either doesn't like or isn't very good at. You'll

create a win-win situation by doing this for a few hours every week while influencing your boss to relieve you of work you don't want to do.

7. *How can I make my boss look good?* One of the best ways to improve your relationship with your boss is to find ways to look good in the eyes of his or her boss and customers. If you can accomplish this, your boss will be much more likely to listen to you and grant your requests.
8. *How can I offer my boss feedback?* As people move up in an organisation, they receive less feedback. In fact, upper managers and CEOs often feel as if they work in a vacuum because they rarely receive clear, honest assessments of their actions. Notice when your boss's work is particularly strong or beneficial to the organisation and give him or her positive feedback and encouragement. Be prepared to offer constructive criticism if asked, but remember that sometimes bosses need a simple, sincere statement of praise for a job well done, just as you do.
9. *What's the best way I can influence my boss?* Many problems with a tough boss result from misunderstandings. Influencing your boss requires good listening skills and some patience. Really listen when your boss outlines expectations and challenges. Regularly ask your boss what he or she expects from you, then summarise back what you've heard. You may feel silly at first, but you will experience far fewer misunderstandings and missed connections. Your boss will feel confident that you have correctly heard what's been said.

Don't stop with your boss: Although these tips are designed specifically for dealing with tough bosses, you can easily apply them in all of your relationships—colleagues, customers, spouses, kids, parents and friends.

Everybody loves to work with somebody who listens, cares and truly takes the time to understand the needs of others. It's an essential part of being a great influencer. Listening in a purposeful, skilled way will give you the opportunity to really know what your boss and co-workers are all about.

9

How to Face Your New Boss

Your boss is the most important individual to work with to achieve success at work. He is a unique individual that can get in a bad mood, make a bad decision, or exhibit imperfections just like anyone else. He can provide you with training, opportunities, and advancement within the organisation. Your new boss will have more impact than anyone else over whether you succeed or fail. Your boss establishes benchmarks for your success, interprets your actions for other key players, and controls resources you need. Building a productive working relationship with him or her while you establish your mandate and negotiate for resources is a clear early priority.

MEETING YOUR BOSSES' STANDARDS

Many young people entering the work force are surprised to learn that their boss is not perfect. Your boss can get in a bad mood, make a bad decision, or exhibit imperfections just like anyone else. The key to achieving success at work is to work around the idiosyncrasies of your boss. Some workers never take the time to understand the requirements of an assignment.

Some bosses just want a quick and dirty job. Some bosses expect everything to be perfect. Some bosses say they just want a quick and dirty job, but when they don't get perfect results, they complain. The solution is to determine the requirements of the assignment and just meet the requirements. Nothing more, nothing less.

Communicate what you need to do your job well. Remember that because your boss may be new to the organisation, he or she may be unaware of your strengths and abilities, so it is important that you make that information available. Keep him or her informed of the assignments you are working on, the decisions you are making, and what reasons you have for making them. Documentation can be a big help in that effort, and it will certainly help keep you organised. If you're the one that's new to the organisation, don't be afraid to tell your boss what resources you feel you need in order to be productive and efficient in your position.

As a rule, you should always strive to seek solutions to problems rather than just push them off onto your boss's desk. Having a good rapport with the boss is quite different from being self-effacing. Speak up if you do not agree or if you have a different point of view. Don't lose your identity in trying to adjust to the boss. Be careful, however, not to overstep the relationship by acting without consulting your boss or by keeping him or her in the dark about your projects.

Often, the changes that a new supervisor brings in can be very positive for your organisation. Look at those changes as opportunities and challenges, and you'll find that working with your new boss is far easier than you anticipated.

ACCOMMODATING BOSSES'S WORK STYLE

Some bosses like to involve them self in your assignment. Some bosses want to make all the decisions, especially when the worker is new and unknown. Some bosses expect you to make all the decisions yourself. They give you an assignment and then make them self scarce so you can't ask any questions. They just want you to get the job done. They don't want to be bothered with the details. Some bosses want to know every little detail of the progress of the assignment.

You need to learn how to accommodate the work style of your boss. It's best to make as many decisions as possible yourself. Keep your boss informed about the progress of your assignment with regular updates. Recognise when the importance of a decision requires you to consult with the boss. Respect your bosses time. If you need help, approach the boss at an opportune moment for the boss and ask when would be a good time to talk. Before you approach the boss for a decision, be prepared to offer possible solutions that the boss might choose from.

Most bosses don't like making decisions. You may think 'that's their job' and perhaps you are right. But bosses love someone who will say, 'I think we should do...xyz* and here's why'. It's a good idea to replace 'xyz' with some genuinely brilliant ideas or you'll find your boss likes you even less.

In meetings, a quick update of where you left off and the key actions you were working on can be critical to a busy boss. Remember you may be 10% or less of their time so make it easy for them to get up to speed with you.

Bosses are busy. When you get an instruction or at the end of a meeting, quickly replay the key decisions and your next actions—then get out of there.

Sometimes we think we are the only person that our boss should be interested in—especially when something is (in our mind) urgent. It can drive you nuts when they don't appear to be interested in your 'urgent' item—but just stop for a minute and ask how important it is. If it's both high on the importance and the urgent ranking then it's time to shout.

If you have a sloppy boss the chances are you will be appreciated much more if you focus on being accurate. If you have a precise boss then the same is true. This is one of those unfair rules but it's no excuse saying that they should be more accurate if you don't take the time to be more precise too.

GETTING FEEDBACK FROM YOUR BOSS

Some bosses are uncomfortable giving a worker feedback, especially if the feedback is negative. Without feedback you can't succeed at work. The solution is to ask your boss for feedback. Ask them how you could have done better on an assignment.

When your boss gives you an assignment, repeat back to them what the expected result of the assignment is and what your first step will be. This will give your boss confidence that you understand the assignment. If there are any areas of the assignment that are unclear, ask questions. You won't appear stupid if you ask questions when you get an assignment, but you will look stupid if you wait until the assignment is almost due to ask a question.

POLITICS AT THE MANAGEMENT LEVEL

It's a fact that all large organisations operate based on politics. Managers collect big salaries, and they don't want to lose that money when they make a mistake. In fact, they strive to make even bigger money by making themselves look good (usually by making someone else look bad). Organisational politics is a complex game of back stabbing and "ass" covering.

At the manager level, playing politics is not a choice, it's a requirement for survival. Although workers are not generally involved in an organisations political game, you can make big points by helping your boss play the game. You do this by making your boss look good.

Never disagree with or confront your boss in public. This will cause them to lose face. If you disagree with your boss, inform them politely in private that you are expressing your opinion to give the boss more information. Let the boss know that despite your disagreement, you intend to carry out your assignment the bosses way.

Some bosses will try to cover their ass by blaming their mistakes on you. Your best response is to just shrug it off. In an organisation, everybody knows who is really responsible when a mistake is made. Some bosses want honest answers. Other bosses want an excuse they can use to cover their ass. Some workers have such good rapport with their boss that they can give them an honest answer along with excuses the boss can use to play the political game.

Never make your boss look bad. Always give advance notice of when you will take time off, and provide a way to cover your responsibilities while you're gone. Try to make your boss look good. In fact, if you accomplish something successful that has high visibility in the organisation, give your boss the credit. Then inform your boss of your career goals.

DEFINING YOUR GOALS

When you think about working with your new boss, keep the following goals in mind:

— *Clarify mutual expectations early*. Begin managing expectations right away. You are in trouble if your boss expects you to fix things fast when you know that the business has serious structural problems. So it is wise to get bad news on the table early and to lower unrealistic expectations. Be careful to assess your new organisation's capacity for change before making ironclad commitments to your new boss.

— *Secure commitments for the resources you need.* In conjunction with establishing goals, begin to negotiate for the key resources—people, funding, and knowledge—you need to succeed. Don't commit to goals without getting corresponding commitments on resources. Otherwise you won't have much bargaining power.

— *Aim for early wins in areas important to the boss.* Whatever your own priorities, identify what the boss cares about most and pursue results in those areas. That way, your boss will feel some ownership of your success. But don't make the mistake of doing things you consider misguided or trivial. In part, your job is to shape your boss's perceptions of what can and should be achieved.

— *Aim for good marks from those whose opinions your boss respects.* This is an aspect of building supportive internal coalitions. Your boss may have pre-existing relationships with people who are now your subordinates. If so, their assessments of you will take on additional importance.

Your relationship with your new boss will be built through a series of conversations.

ESTABLISHING HOW YOU WILL WORK TOGETHER

It's essential to figure out how you and your boss will work together. Your preferences may differ, such as over how much information the boss wants (and you want to give) and how involved the boss wants to be (and you want him or her to be) in the details of what you are doing. Rather than allowing misunderstandings to complicate your relationship, spend some time at the start discussing how you will work together. Even if you don't develop a close personal bond, doing so will help you create a productive working relationship.

MATCHING YOUR REQUESTS FOR SUPPORT

The type of support you need from your boss will vary depending on the business situation you are facing. The role of the boss in a startup is very different than in turnaround, realignment, or sustaining success situations. So you need to gain consensus on the type of situation. Then you have to think carefully about what role you would like your new boss to play and what kinds of support you will ask for.

The table below summarises typical roles that new bosses play in each of the four major types of transition situations.

Situation	*Typical Roles for the New Boss*
Startup	Helping to get critically important resources quickly.
	Setting clear, measurable goals.
	Lots of up-front attention, then get out of the way.
	Guidance at key strategic breakpoints.
	Help in staying focused.
Turnaround	Same as startup plus:
	More support for making and implementing the tough personnel calls.
	Support for changing or correcting the external image of the organisation and its people.
	Helping the new leader cut deep enough early enough.

Realignment	Same as startup plus: Helping the new leader make the case for change to the organisation, especially if he or she is coming in from the outside.
Sustaining Success	Constant reality testing: is this truly a sustaining success situation or a realignment? Support for playing good defence, not making mistakes that damage the business. Help in finding ways to take the business to a new level.

LIVING BY THE GOLDEN RULE

Do unto others as you would have them do unto you. You will almost certainly hire new people as your subordinates. Just as you need to develop a productive relationship with your new boss, they need to work effectively with you. In the past, have you done a good job of helping subordinates make their own transitions? What might you do differently this time?

PLANNING FOR FIVE CONVERSATIONS

Your relationship with your new boss will be built through a series of conversations These conversations begin before you accept the new position and continue through the time before entry and on into your transition. It is critically important that you cover certain fundamental subjects in these conversations. In fact, it is worth planning for five distinct conversations with your new boss:

— *The situational diagnosis conversation.* In this conversation you seek to understand how your new boss sees the business situation. Is it a turnaround or a startup or a realignment or a sustaining success situation? How did the organisation get to this point? What are the relevant factors—both soft and hard—that make this a challenge? What resources within the organisation do you have to draw upon? Naturally your view may be different than your boss's, but it essential that you understand how he or she sees the situation.

— *The expectations conversation*. In this conversation you seek to understand and negotiate expectations. What are the few key things that your new boss needs you to accomplish in the short-term and medium term? What will constitute success? When? How will it be measured? Here again, you may come to believe that your boss's expectations are unrealistic and have to work to reset them. Also you should take care, as part of your broader effort to secure early wins, to under-promise and over-deliver.

— *The style conversation*. In this conversation you work to understand how you and your new boss can best interact on an ongoing basis. How does she prefer to be communicated with? Face-to-face? In writing? By voice mail or e-mail? How often? What kinds of decisions does he want to be involved in and where can you make the call on your own? How do your styles differ and what are the implications for how you should interact?

— *The resources conversation*. In this conversation you negotiate for critical resources. What is it that you need to be successful? What do you need your boss to do? The resources in question need not be funding or personnel. In a realignment situation, for example, your boss can play a critical role in helping you get the organisation to confront the need for change.

— *The personal development conversation*. Finally, you need to discuss how your time in this job will contribute to your personal development. Are there projects or special assignments that you could get involved in? Are there courses or programmes that would strengthen your capabilities?

In practice, these five conversations are interwoven and take place over time. But there is a sequential logic. Early conversations should focus on situational diagnosis, expectations, and style. As you learn more, you can move to resources, revisiting situation and expectations as necessary. When you feel the relationship is reasonably well established, you can begin the personal development conversation.

TIPS TO SURVIVE YOUR NEW BOSS

Just when you're used to a comfortable routine, along comes a new boss with new ideas and new ways of working and it's all change. How do you make sure that you're exactly the sort of candidate he or she would have hired in the first place? Here are 16 tips to make sure you survive:

1. *Tune in to your boss's working style.* Arrange a meeting to find out how things will be run. New leaders naturally want to make their mark, so you'll need to help your new boss translate his or her vision and ideas.
2. *Project positive energy.* At a time of change, everyone feels unsettled so no one wants to listen to a whinger. Be a motivator: the person everyone wants to be around.
3. *Get early feedback.* Ask for feedback halfway through your first task or project to make sure you've correctly understood what's needed and that you're on the right track.
4. *Understand how you'll be evaluated.* Know precisely on which skills, behaviours and accomplishments

you will be judged and rewarded. Focus on them like a laser.

5. *Be dependable.* Do what you say you're going to do. Better still, under-promise and over-deliver.
6. *Make your boss look good.* Finish your work on time and with a high level of professionalism. Bring new ideas to your boss and offer to take charge and implement them.
7. *Think on your own two feet.* Don't run to the boss with every question you have or setback you encounter. If you must report a problem, develop possible solutions to present.
8. *Be courteous.* Show respect and loyalty to your boss and speak well of him or her to others.
9. *Go beyond the call of duty.* Take on added challenges, put in extra hours and be a team player.
10. *Be enthusiastic.* As soon as you finish a project, ask if there are other things you can start.
11. *Take your style cues from your boss.* It is better to dress too smart than too casual.
12. *Make an effort with your appearance.* It suggests that you will make an effort at work.
13. *Punctuality is more than just manners.* Always be on time if not a few minutes early. Being late suggests you can't really be bothered.
14. *Come prepared.* Far too many people arrive at meetings under-prepared, so this is one easy way to gain adoration from above.
15. *Be known.* Communicating in person—rather than e-mail—whenever possible is imperative for success-seekers, no matter how intimidating or unaccommodating your boss may be.

16. *Stay up-to-date.* The business landscape is fast-changing. Those who stay current, keeping their skills and thinking fresh will be regarded as valuable and important team members.
17. *Deliver the goods.* In business, it's all about accountability. If for whatever reason you have fallen short in a task, admit it. Take responsibility for the shortfall and show willing to resolve it. The boss will respect your approach.

If you have a new boss in your current job, you need to focus on building a solid working relationship. Right now, this is the most important person in your work life. He or she can be the most influential champion for your career, so it's essential to get off to a good start—and stay in their good books.

10

How to Influence Your Boss

One of the toughest tasks for an employee is learning to lead up, influencing your boss to follow you. There are many challenges you face. The first one is the differential in positional power, the simple fact that who you are seeking to influence is above you in the pecking order and usually expects you to be the one doing the following. The second challenge you face is overcoming any self-doubt that you may have about your own judgement. The third difficulty is the degree of risk you take on when you stick your neck out and speak up by offering direction or correction to someone above you in the hierarchy. Another challenge lies in accurately assessing the degree of your supervisor's openness or willingness to receive feedback. Finally, you face the challenge of swimming against the tide of deference to authority that is expected of us in organisations of every stripe and persuasion.

How do you become a highly valued employee which your employer feel is indispensible? By being mindful of the following tips, you will get that promotion and bonus. These tips are not out of the world and in fact, by applying them consistently, they save you much time and effort.

1. *Do not drop the bombshell at the last minute.* Take it from me, bosses do not like surprises. Even if it is a bad news, break it to them early so that they have time to react and can be prepared. Dropping bombshells at the last minute work against you. People get stressed, tempers flare and people act rashly. It is that ticking timebomb within all of us that gets fired up when we are stressed. So do your boss a favour and try to avoid dropping the bombshell at the last minute. There is a difference between trying to solve a problem independently and highlighting an issue early.
2. *Be the problem solver, not problem creator.* Everyone loves a problem solver. Inherent in human is the lazy bug that sets in. Make things as easy as possible for your boss and they'll love you. Imagine how much more appreciative a boss will be, knowing that someone has done the thinking for him. Now all your boss has to do is to input his additional insight and trust me, this is often well-appreciated. By doing this, you have demonstrated initiative and the right professional work ethic that all of them will love.
3. *Get your "brag" sheet on real time.* Dread the time where you have to do a appraisal with your boss? Well, instead of dreading it, you should make the full use of this opportunity. Whip out your "brag" sheet. You've done the job, so it is your bragging right to highlight the great works you have done. Always remember the acronym S.M.A.R.T. Be smart in your work, show a brag sheet that provides evidence of your results which are in line with your goals that are specific, measurable, attainable, realistic and timely.
4. *Your call for action.* Take control of your professional destiny. These are the rules for success at work and

in life. Learn them well and they in turn, will serve you well.

PRINCIPLES TO INFLUENCE OTHERS

There are six widely used successful principles of influence:

1. *Reciprocation*. People are more willing to comply with requests from those who have provided such things first.
2. *Commitment and consistency*. People are more willing to be moved in a particular direction if they see it as consistent with an existing or recently-made commitment. For instance, high pressure door-to-door sales companies are plagued by the tendency of some buyers to cancel the deal after the salesperson has left and the pressure to buy is no longer present.
3. *Authority*. People are more willing to follow the directions or recommendations of someone they view as an authority.
4. *Social validation*. People are more willing to take a recommended step if they see evidence that many others, especially similar others, are taking it. Manufacturers make use of this principle by claiming that their product is the fastest growing or largest selling in the market. The strategy of increasing compliance by providing evidence of others who had already complied was the most widely used of the six principles he encountered.
5. *Scarcity*. People find objects and opportunities more attractive to the degree that they are scarce, rare, or dwindling in availability. Hence, newspaper ads are filled with warnings to potential customers regarding the folly of delay: "Last three days."

"Limited time offer." "One week only sale." One particularly single-minded movie theatre owner who managed to load three separate appeals to the scarcity principle into just five words of advertising copy that read, "Exclusive, limited engagement, ends soon."

6. *Liking and friendship.* People prefer to say yes to those they know and like.

INFLUENCE AND POWER

The currency of politics in any corporation isn't money; it's influence. The culture at the top of nearly every organisation is power-based. But that's not power in the sense of raw strength. Power in organisational cultures is based on influence over key decisions, especially those that deal with allocating resources and choosing of people for important positions. Winning that power, then keeping it, is essential to getting your own way.

Influence gives a boss the power of patronage: the power to give chosen people a leg-up; the power to bestow rewards — or withhold them as punishment. The more influence you have, the more real power you wield. Fancy titles and big offices may *look* impressive, but they mean next to nothing without the influence to get what you want done. Indeed, these material shows of hierarchy are often given to losers in the influence game as consolation prizes to repair some of the damage to their egos. After all, you may still need their support one day. The successful politician never humiliates an opponent — unless that opponent can be removed totally from any further involvement in the business.

Essential Influence

Influence matters most in the game of executive politics. Without influence, you have nothing. With enough of it, you're the person everyone seeks out and tries to please. Essential Influence is whatever produces the impact needed to get your ideas accepted and your people into important positions. The Law of Essential Influence states that gaining and keeping this necessary influence is the primary task of every executive who wants to get to the top and stay there.

As influence produces power, so greater power increases influence. *To him that hath, more shall be given.* Anyone who has little influence will soon lose whatever he or she has. If you can't win and keep the essential amount of influence, you'll have no power. And in a power culture, losing your power is like losing all your money. You'll have to beg and hope others will throw you scraps. You won"t be able to affect important decisions. The people who looked to you for advancement will be disappointed and whatever title you hold will be meaningless. Everyone will know you're a loser. You'll be a nobody.

All this means that you have to show your boss how your idea will increase his or her Essential Influence in the organisation. To do this, you need to:

— Think about the likely political impact of the idea at least as much as you consider its technical or creative merits. It may be brilliant, but if it's *only* brilliant, you'll have a tough job to get your boss to do much with it.

— In any presentation, give at least as much time to explaining how much others will benefits from the idea as you do to how good the idea is. Whoever controls an idea with a good pay-off has a powerful source of fresh patronage at his or her disposal.

— Try to talk privately to any contacts you have in key departments in advance. Get them interested. Then let your boss know that others are already sniffing around what promises to be a popular idea. Not only will this help convince the boss that your idea is a likely winner, it will start her thinking that, if she doesn't take charge of the ideas, her colleagues might just beat her to the punch and grab that influence for themselves.

— Suggest to the boss that he tries the idea out on influential colleagues, while you get on with the nuts and bolts. He's going to do this anyway, but it never hurts to show that you understand corporate realities.

Law of Mutual Impact

The law of mutual impact is a cornerstone of corporate politics. Put simply, it says whatever one executive says or does affects all the others — without exception. Below senior levels, your actions don't impact others to the same extent. Junior managers have their own responsibilities and can exercise them with relative freedom. They may even have limited power to make decisions others must follow. It's prudent for them to consult before taking action, but it isn't always essential.

As you get nearer the top, there are **no** decisions you can make alone. Everything is subject to the Law of Mutual Impact. All your colleagues have a deep, pressing interest in whatever you do or say. Assuming she can act alone is a cardinal political sin and will quickly get your boss into serious trouble. Consultation before action isn't simply good manners, or prudent, it's *essential*. Your boss's colleagues won't thank her for acting without notice, especially if what you have persuaded her to do embarrasses them or causes them to lose face. They believe its their absolute right to influence every colleague's decisions to avoid causing *them* problems. Superiors praise decisive action and initiative, so it's natural to believe higher-level jobs will have the greatest freedom of action and the most direct personal authority. Neither statement is correct. Perfect freedom of action is a myth. What freedom there is at the top — and it's more limited than you might think — is shared by the executive group as a whole, not held by any individual member. Because of the Law of Mutual Impact, top executives have to consult their colleagues on *everything*.

What this means in managing your boss is:

— You must give him or her enough time to consult. Never spring a need for a decision at the last moment. Never try to push action forward by asking the boss to go out on a limb. Only a fool ever does this, and I'm going to assume your boss isn't one of those.

— Never place your boss in an embarrassing position in front of colleagues. Whatever differences you may have, keep them private to a time when you and she are alone. If your boss is suspected of having a "loose cannon" amongst her team, her colleagues are going to start watching her too carefully for comfort. It will also be taken as a sign of management weakness.

— Make sure you brief you boss really well for the consultation process. Nothing will kill your idea faster than the boss raising it with an important colleague, then being asked a question he wasn't prepared for. It not only makes him feel an idiot, it makes him suspect you've sent him off to talk to others about an idea that you haven't fully thought through yourself. That will put a big hole in your credibility.

— Whatever your boss promises — however much you wish he had kept his mouth shut and his brain in gear — never make it clear that the promise was either empty or impossible to honour. His senior colleagues must trust that he can deliver, or they will fear he is putting their positions at risk. If he's got himself into a hole, keep quiet and help get him out. He'll remember it. If you leave him to get himself out, he'll remember that for much longer.

— Never try to short-circuit the process by talking to senior people about your idea yourself. It passes a strong message that you suspect your boss isn't keeping them informed properly. If they believe that, he or she is dead meat. And, when the boss finds out, so are you.

TURNING YOUR BOSS INTO A PARTNER

Building a better working relationship with your boss can unlock a variety of future possibilities, from promotion to easier interactions and bigger bonuses. In some cases, your chances for future advancement may be improved by helping the boss become more effective with his or her higher-ups. By gaining influence with your boss, you can build a relationship and create benefits for you both. Too many managers and leaders make poor bosses, and the good ones could be even better. What may come as a surprise, however, is how much your boss's effectiveness relies on you. It's part of your job to make the boss a better manager.

Recognising that the boss needs your assistance, like a senior partner needs the help of a junior partner, you can move the basic nature of your dealings with the boss away from the old superior-subordinate form of interaction. While a difference in hierarchy remains, junior and senior partners collaborate to tackle challenges, solve problems and achieve common goals. By putting yourself in the shoes of a partner, you can avoid common pitfalls that can hurt your chances for success:

withholding important information, forgetting the boss's needs or competing with the boss rather than helping. Think of yourself as your boss's junior partner, not just a subordinate.

How do junior partners act? They don't let their partners:

— Make huge mistakes

— Inadvertently look bad

— Go uninformed when you know things the partner should know.

Partners do:

— Stay loyal to the partnership's objectives

— Place the good of the organisation ahead of their own good

— Value and take advantage of differing skills and perspectives

— Tolerate each other's foibles.

Not assume that bad behaviour comes from bad intentions but rather from misinformation or misguided views. No self-respecting partner could stand silently by when other partners, no matter how senior, are about to make a costly blunder, overlook important opportunities, or miss vital information that could affect success. It is the obligation of a partner to be as responsible as possible, even at the risk of personal discomfort or embarrassment. This asks a lot of you, but wouldn't you want that kind of basic mindset from the people who report to you? Accept responsibility for the relationship with your boss; both of you have a stake in your being more productive. That is the leverage point for influence with your manager. By becoming the boss's junior partner, you can build influence that in turn can bring you the kinds of benefits many people want: greater scope to your job; better supervision and coaching; a closer or more open work relationship; even a boss who is more effective in the organisation.

Here's a model to follow to begin developing a partnership relationship with your boss. There are four main things to pay attention to:

1. See the boss as a potential ally (a partner).
2. Make sure you really understand the boss's world.
3. Be aware of the resources (currencies) you already have, or can acquire.
4. Pay attention to how the boss wants to be related to.

Let's take a well-known, dramatic example. Is your boss as demanding as Donald Trump? Do you experience him as highly judgemental, jumping on you when you make the slightest mistake? Do you want him to help you develop? Before writing him off as totally impossible, assume that he might be a potential ally, a partner who is very concerned about success and deeply worried about failure. With that orientation, maybe you won't just cringe at his comments but look for what you can learn from them.

Want to influence a person like Trump? First, see him as a potential ally and partner and try to understand his world: New York real estate. It's a cutthroat industry in a competitive city, with very large fortunes made—and lost, even by Trump. With those pressures, Trump probably won't be very patient with subordinates. He needs to know his people are the best at what they do, that they're savvy, skilful dealmakers and not necessarily business managers. Likely currencies he values: street smarts, financial acumen, reliability, toughness, ability to spot big opportunities, and thoroughness.

Next, examine what you offer. Assuming you have basic financial knowledge, you control your effort level, your analytical thoroughness, and how tough and tough-minded you are. Can you be as nervy as he would like, to make him confident in your bold thinking? Can you hunt down deals with the pros? Then consider how he interacts with others—clients and business associates. Is he usually gruff and blunt? And how does he respond to people who are forceful rather than deferential? He may respect those who stand up to him.

Influence Strategy

We can't guarantee that this way of talking will work, but it has a chance because it follows three central principles:

— *Show your boss how it is in his interest to change his behaviour.* Notice the difference between saying that you want him to help develop you because it will make you happy, and wanting development because it emphasises the return on his investment, which he cares a lot about.

— *Show your boss that it is in his interest for you to be successful and satisfied, since it will get the best work from you.* While acknowledging your interests, you're connecting right back to what he wants.

— *Deliver your preference in a compatible style that is preferred by your boss.* You've used a tough, no-nonsense tone, asserting that you can take anything he dishes out, and want to, but made it clear that the effort will be more productive if he bothers to think about your learning.

The idea is to always be on the side of your boss, not an antagonist or critic. You are always seeking to help the boss meet his or her goals.

By partnering with your boss, you can shape the quality of supervision you receive, improve your own development and encourage the sort of coaching that you want. Some workers lament a lack of coaching from the boss, citing a "sink or swim" attitude. Others cite an apparent lack of attention from a boss who appears to be overworked or preoccupied and only chimes in with quick criticisms. Still others complain of an opposite problem—the over attentive boss who gets too involved in the details and impedes independent action. In all three cases, the problem stems from ineffective communication. You need to find a way to talk to your boss to convey not only your need for coaching or leeway, but also to show why that effort will be good for the organisation overall.

As your boss's partner, you have an obligation to be forthcoming when you have needed information. On many issues, you automatically have information that can be useful. For example, you know what impact the boss is having on you and, often, on your peers. You may also know how the boss is seen further down in the organisation, in other units, and possibly by some of his or her colleagues and superiors. In addition, you may have some skills that your boss does not. Knowledge in any of these areas can be invaluable to a manager.

Often, it seems to require great courage to tell your boss that there is something he or she could do more effectively, or to offer help. But if you show that you really care about your boss's effectiveness, and you step forward in this positive spirit of partnership, then many bosses will be more grateful than resentful. Part of why it is "lonely at the top" is because so few subordinates see that bosses need to learn and grow, too. Good bosses appreciate the person who is willing to be helpful. The exchange of information about performance, is a beneficial exchange that is too seldom executed.

Suggested Readings

Alan R. Schonberg, Robert L. Shook, Donna G. Estreicher, *169 Ways to Score Points With Your Boss*, McGraw-Hill, 1998.

Carol Hymowitz, "When You Disagree With the Boss's Order, Do You Tell Your Staff?" *Wall Street Journal*, April 16, 2002.

Carol Hymowitz, "How Managers Can Keep from Being Ambushed by the Boss," *Wall Street Journal*, April 9, 2002.

Gini Graham Scott, *A Survival Guide for Working With Bad Bosses: Dealing With Bullies, Idiots, Back-stabbers, And Other Managers from Hell*, AMACOM, November 25, 2005.

Jack Stack and Bo Burlingham, *A Stake in the Outcome: Building a Culture of Ownership for the Long-Term Success of Your Business*, Currency Doubleday, 2002.

Jack Stack and Bo Burlingham, *The Great Game of Business*, Currency Doubleday, 1994.

Joseph L. Badaracco, Jr., *Leading Quietly: An Unorthodox Guide to Doing the Right Thing*, Harvard Business School Press, 2002.

Michael Useem, *Leading Up: How to Lead Your Boss So You Both Win*, Crown Business, 2001.

Ros Jay, *How to Manage Your Boss: Developing the Perfect Working Relationship*, Financial Times Management, June 2002.

Roger Fritz, *How to Manage Your Boss*, Career Pr Inc; 2 edition October 1994.

Tim Frazier and Dana Frazier, *Boss: Management Tips for Today from a Nineteenth Century Cattle Drive*, Abilene: McWhiney Foundation Press, 2006.

Index

Other Books on

GENERAL SERIES

1.	Art of Joyful Living **(New)**	160/-
2.	Chanakya Neeti **(New)**	175/-
3.	Helpline for Stressed Parents **(New)**	175/-
4.	Grow Rich with Peace of Mind **(New)**	175/-
5.	How to be Fit and Young **(New)**	175/-
6.	How to Succeed in Life **(New)**	175/-
7.	100 Ways to Develop Self Confidence	175/-
8.	Child Development	225/-
9.	Abraham Lincoln A Complete Biography	225/-
10.	Mein Kampf My Struggle	225/-
11.	Think and Grow Rich	160/-
12.	The Art of Personality Development	150/-
13.	Positive Mind Power	160/-
14.	Travel & Tourism An Industry Facilitator	295/-
15.	World's Great Authors And Poets	150/-
16.	Effective Editing Help Yourself in Becoming a Good Editor	150/-
17.	Smart House-Keeping for Modern Women	195/-
18.	Develop Super Power Memory	175/-
19.	World's Great Personalities	195/-
20.	Personality Plus	150/-
21.	Power of Positive Thinking	160/-
22.	Art of Successful Parenting	225/-
23.	A Handbook of Etiquettes	125/-
24.	World's Great Scientists	195/-
25.	Body Language	175/-
26.	Art of Successful Living	175/-
27.	Jokes for All	150/-
28.	Selected Dohas	350/-
29.	Baby Names for Girls **(New)**	150/-
30.	Baby Names for Boys **(New)**	150/-
31.	Art of Public Speaking	160/-
32.	The World's Greatest Speeches	175/-
33.	Group Discussions	125/-
34.	Personality Development	125/-
35.	Think Positive & Things Will Go Right	125/-
36.	Once in a Blue Moon (A Tantra Tale)	125/-
37.	God is Dead	125/-
38.	Travel India (A Complete Guide for Tourists)	350/-
39.	Glimpses of Urdu Poetry	450/-
40.	How to Reduce Tension	125/-
41.	A Book of Stenography	295/-
42.	Baby Names for the Boy	150/-
43.	Baby Names for the Girl	150/-
44.	Ripples in Tranquil Waters	195/-

Lotus PRESS

Unit No. 220, 2nd Floor, 4735/22, Prakash Deep Building,
Ansari Road, Darya Ganj, New Delhi- 110002
Ph.: 23280047, 9811594448
• E-mail : lotuspress1984@gmail.com, www.lotuspress.co.in